JULY 4, 1776.

States of Ameri

I0558237

JOY MARIE IBSEN

THE DECLARATION

of

Interdependence

Equality and Democracy!

"..I have just received and devoured
your new book.. I found it unputdownable.
You have distilled a lifetimes' experiences
and wisdom into a book for all times,
and I am truly interdependent with you as a result.
It is a fascinating journey, looking into the
rear-view mirror while still driving! Above
and beyond all your wisdom-- and I especially
enjoyed *Racial Just Us*-- I learned a good deal more
about you. Thank you so much for this
endearing and enriching gift."

**~Edward Broadbridge, Translator and Editor, 6
volumes, N.F.S. Grundtvig, Aarhus University Press**

The Declaration of *Inter*dependence

Joy Marie Ibsen

The Declaration of *Inter*dependence

By Joy Marie Ibsen

Co-creating a new
world: fully, freely,
and happily loving
life!

To my children,

Thea, Mitch and Noah,
I love you and am so
blessed to be your
mom.

508 West 26th Street KEARNEY, NE 68848
402-819-3224
info@medialiteraryexcellence.com

*INTER*DEPENDENCE

"Injustice anywhere is a threat to justice everywhere. We are caught in an inescapable network of mutuality, tied in a single garment of destiny. Whatever affects one directly, affects all indirectly.
I can never be what I ought to be until you are what you ought to be. This is the interrelated structure of reality."

Dr. Martin Luther King

"The earth does not belong to man; man belongs to the earth. All things are connected like the blood that unites us all. Man did not weave the web of life; he is merely a strand in it. Whatever he does to the web, he does to himself."

Chief Seattle

"We can either emphasize those aspects of our traditions, religious or secular, that spark hatred, exclusion and suspicion, or work with those that stress the interdependence and equality of all human beings. The choice is yours."

Karen Armstrong

"Human First, then Christian."

N.F.S. Grundtvig

"Interdependence is and ought to be as much the ideal of man as self- sufficiency. Man is a social being. "

Mahatma Gandhi

"Our own survival is so dependent on the help of others that a need for love lies at the very core of
our existence. "

His Holiness, the Dahli Lama

"An experience of life without faith and without love is full of separateness and thus full of pain."

Sai Maa

"Love the Lord your God with all your heart and with all your soul and with all your mind and with all your strength. The second is this: 'Love your neighbor as yourself.' There is no commandment greater than these."

Jesus (Mark 12:30-31 NIV)

"We are all better off when we are all better off."

Anonymous

TABLE OF CONTENTS

PART I

EQUALITY

PART II

Grundtvig's Four Principles, Folk Schools, Civil Rights

PART III

PROSE POEMS

Preface

Equality

This book is about the essential equality of all humanity, the cornerstone of the Declaration of Independence.

Without recognizing our common equality, we cannot fulfill our country's purpose as stated in the Declaration of Independence.

To be Independent, we must be *Inter*dependent.

In order to achieve *Inter*dependence, we need to recognize the equality of all human beings and treat each other accordingly.

We must reclaim the true meaning of our inalienable rights— life, liberty and the pursuit of happiness—terms which have had their meaning distorted, their power weakened, and no longer connote the essential equality of all people beyond our prejudicial filters of racism, ethnicity, gender, financial status, social class or other personal traits. We have much to correct and much to gain!

This book is divided into three parts.

Part 1 is about the problems we experience due to inequality. Unfortunately, the meanings of our basic rights have often been misused in restrictive ways, with derisive effects, deterring equality.

Sixteen "real life" stories are presented which explore inequality. The stories are from my own experiences. The incidents may be extremely mild compared to what the reader may have directly experienced in terms of prejudicial acts of racism, ethnicity, social class, gender and other modes of projecting inequality. The intention is not to compete in how painful or damaging acts of prejudice can be, but rather to share experiences and explore the aftermath of what happens, the harm it does, how we feel when it happens, ways we sometimes contribute to it, and what we can do to prevent it in the first place. Recognizing causes and changing inappropriate responses make our world a better place.

Part II introduces Walter Capps, a professor who identified four basic principles to help bring unity among people of all backgrounds, independent of all religions, leading to a world where there are more values in common. The straightforward principles of N.F.S Grundtvig[1] a Danish philosopher, educator and poet are each explored as a path toward more egalitarianism. Denmark continuously receives top ratings for its large majority of happy and healthy people. The United States is not Denmark and vice versa, but Denmark has a capitalistic economy with a democratic government where both liberal and conservative parties acknowledge Grundtvig's influences.

The four principles in the Folk Schools which were founded by Grundtvig help people enjoy life, be educated, and empower them for democracy. Folk school practices in Africa, Asia and Europe (including third world countries) are presented. Many people in the United States are not aware of Myles Horton and the significant contributions of Highlander Folk School to the Civil Rights movement. The United States has benefited greatly from the rich folk school legacy as evidenced in the speech from President Barack Obama at a state dinner honoring Nordic leaders.

Part III takes a completely different approach. Prose Poetry, which requires slower reading and deeper thought, is used to express matters of heart and head on the subjects of Equality, Democracy, Interdependence, Independence, Justice, Freedom

---

[1] *Biographical information and a statement about N.F.S Grundtvig's influence can be found in "Grundtvig in America," by Joy Ibsen, See Appendix.*

and Truth. An example:

EQUALITY

Every person in the United States,

Each soul on earth,

is equal to every other soul:

equal spirits equal

equal people.

We are distinct individuals,

differing in age, size, race,

religion, gender, ethnicity,

class, finances, beliefs,

goals, abilities, looks,

tastes, manners, style.

THE DECLARATION OF *INTER*DEPENDENCE

We all belong to the same source.

Each of us is part of one

fabulous whole.

Unequivocally,

interconnected.

Humanity is comprised of billions of people.

Like snowflakes, one in a trillion, a trillion in one,

souls being human,

snowflakes being snow.

Blessed are the losers;

they shall be winners.

Blessed are the winners;

they shall be losers.

We're all in this together.

Ours is a world

we all share—

one universal

public park.

Every litter bit hurts.

Introduction

The Declaration of Independence clearly states the major purpose of the United States of America---to establish a country based on equality, a model for humanity living peacefully together, honoring one's own and one another's sacred rights! A divine experiment![2]

Our purpose is to create a society designed by the people, for the people, and of the people. It is called a democracy. We are still very much in process and now in a critical, perhaps all-or-nothing state as to whether or not we can succeed.

Critics of our democracy point out that our founding fathers and mothers supported major limitations regarding equality. Our nation's founders were unsuccessful in establishing a model of equality in their daily lives much less establishing equality in the entire country. Many of our founders had slaves. Women were considered unworthy of having a vote!

Yes, that is true! The work toward establishing more equality continues, influenced by the belief that the United States has a divine purpose—establishing a model country based on equality for the entire globe. Understanding equality and continuing to increase its presence throughout society is the primary measure for successfully fulfilling our place in human history. While many barriers remain, consider the progress that we've made!

We no longer have slaves! Many progenies of slaves are independent; many have made and continue to make valuable contributions to our society. While racial prejudice is still rampant, the celebration of intermarriage and bi-racial families has become

---

[2] *Grundtvig's famous aphorism that humans are not apes but a "divine experiment" is in the Prologue to Nordic Mythology, translated in vol 1, The School for Life (2011)*

commonplace and acceptable. Not so long ago, that was impossible.

Immigrants from a huge array of ethnic and religious backgrounds came to this country nearly empty handed and now have lives which their great -great grandparents could only dream of. Ethnic groups which were sometimes treated as inferior and unfit to be citizens of the United States, now have major roles in business and government.

Women not only vote but are increasingly gaining more income equality. The day will definitely come when we have a woman president. The strengths and contributions to society of both women and men are increasingly honored by both sexes. Gender equality is not yet here but it is a future reality.

We will continue to grow in understanding and acceptance of gender equality. In the United States we now have same-sex marriage equality as a constitutional right. Much more progress is needed, especially in terms of transgender issues.

Recently gains in equality, such as same-sex marriage, and arguments over the handling of transgender issues seem to inspire attempts to erode democracy. Incorrect assertions are made without being retracted or stopped. Truths are sometimes used to cover lies. (An example is using the goal of equality as a rationale to no longer teach facts about history, the racial inequality which has existed, still exists and continues to damage this country!) Lies are repeated over and over with the intent that repetition will qualify the lies as truths.

Unfortunately, the meaning of words describing our inalienable rights—life, liberty and the pursuit of happiness—have become distorted due to misleading or wrongful associations. We will examine this in more detail later, but briefly, "Life" is associated with "Right to Life." The phrase sounds like it is associated with freedom, but it refers to the elimination of freedom for thousands of women. It is a hijacking of the literal meaning of the words. There was a time when the "Right to Life" referred to having a full, happy life. Now the expression is commonly used to mean the right to birth. Whatever your position on abortion, this was not the meaning the writers of the Declaration of Independence had in mind.

"Liberty" (Freedom) has also been redefined. Too many people understand the words liberty or freedom as the right to do anything a person wishes without regard to the rights of others or the effects on them. This is not what freedom means.

"Pursuit of Happiness" has not changed its literal definition, but its meaning has changed due to advertisements and social pressures equating happiness with endless acquisition of material goods, attainment of power, or notoriety. Happiness does not come from having excessive goods, fame, receiving rewards, or acquiring power. Happiness comes from having loving relationships with others and by following one's purpose in life.

Let's proceed to honor and protect the essential equality of all people, and reconnect with each other as we explore our own and each other's inalienable rights.

First, we need to recognize the basic, essential equality of all people and our interdependence on one another. By definition, there is plenty of equality for everyone to share!

THE DECLARATION OF INDEPENDENCE

"We hold these truths to be self-evident, that all human beings are created equal, that they are endowed by their Creator with certain inalienable rights, which among them are life, liberty and the pursuit of happiness."

THE DECLARATION OF *INTER*INDEPENDENCE

"We hold these truths to be self-evident, that all human beings are created equal without regard to race, gender, ethnicity, social position, financial status, handicaps or other identifying group characteristics; all human beings are endowed by their Creator with certain inalienable rights, which among them are the right to live fully, freely, and in pursuit of true happiness."

PART I

EQUALITY

Equality

All human beings are essentially equal. We are all one.

For almost two hundred and fifty years our nation has struggled with the concept of equality, too often emphasizing differences and judging certain groups of human beings as inferior. The quality of our lives and our successful evolution as human beings depends on the degree to which we acknowledge and accept one another's differences and practice the oneness of all humanity.

THE DECLARATION OF *INTER*DEPENDENCE

The Declaration of *Inter*dependence simply adds specifics to the Declaration of Independence, further clarifying the specific areas of equality, and our purposeful role of creating a nation where all can live fully, freely and pursue true happiness.

Inter means between, among, mutually reciprocal. Interdependence is a dependence which is reciprocal and mutual, a dependence between and among us. We depend on each other for strength, knowledge, love, help, and for meaning in our lives.

The Declaration of Interdependence is not an official, governmental, congressional or historic document. It is simply a way to examine the true nature of the Declaration of Independence, restore the intended meaning and honor this sacred document.

Independence can only occur when it is rooted in *Inter*dependence. It is that simple! Only *Inter*dependence brings independence into being. My life, my health, my world depends on how I relate to and affect others, and how others relate to and affect me. We cannot possibly live fully, freely and in the pursuit of real happiness if we do not first understand the basic equality we share with every human being.

Our Pledge to Human Equality

We believe in universal human equality. We celebrate life and commit ourselves to fairness for all people. We appreciate human diversity, honor each other's religion, race and ethnicity, and reject the lowering of anyone's essential worth based on religion, race, ethnicity, gender, age, financial status, handicaps, social class, or similar factors of labeling. We accept the divergence of views and delight in the great variety of humanity. We support human ingenuity and life-long education. We believe every human being has inalienable rights to life, liberty and the pursuit of happiness. Together, we will work together for the common good, listening to one another, comparing thoughts, expressing kindness, caring for each other and caring for the earth. We are all one.

The Inalienable Right to Live Life

In the United States "the right to life," or "pro-life" has unfortunately, come to mean anti-abortion. It is not a term used to describe support for anti-war sentiment or anti-death sentences for prisoners on death row, nor is it a term used to support the movement, "Black Lives Matter." The term "right to life" sounds as if it describes freedom, but it is restrictive in its meaning and can now have serious criminal consequences. It does not imply celebrating life itself. The term implies more pain and tears rather than joy and celebration!

By successfully equating the right to life as prohibiting pre-birth abortion, a cloud of potential evil-doing is cast on women, especially those who have had abortions (not the men involved). It has unpleasant implications for all women.

The term abortion did not exist in the hearts or minds of the men formulating the Declaration of Independence, nor those who wrote and passed the Constitution of the United States, (or wrote the Bible for that matter). The subject was considered a private matter and not publicly discussed.

The Supreme Court's 2022 decision to determine the illegality of abortion a matter of individual state laws is an abuse of power. Our country recognizes freedom of religion. Only a minority of our nation's religions consider abortion an evil act, and while their religious beliefs are allowable, they should not be thrust on those who do not share that belief. Punishable criminal sentences or lack of appropriate medical care should not affect millions of people who believe that abortion is not a sinful abomination, but often a matter of personal health, welfare and one's own faith.

Whatever one believes, a more accurate term is not "the

right to life," but rather "the right to birth." there is a lot more to the meaning of the word "life" than the right to be born. The right to life means the right to live life fully—through childhood, adulthood, old age and perhaps beyond. The "right to birth" is a different matter. One has the right to believe abortion (to prevent birth) is wrong. However, one's state address should not determine the legality of abortion. Ours is a country where there is religious freedom; millions of religious people, in the United States, including leaders, do not consider abortion criminal.

Abortion is a matter for those directly involved to make a decision that will affect them—only the woman, man, health practitioner involved, and the individuals they invite to help make their decision. It is a very serious matter.

Life is much more than the right to birth. Life is a daily adventure. Life is experiencing this gorgeous and wondrous planet! Life is learning about oneself, others, our world and beyond! Life is about being a human being, not being a machine.

Life is loving and caring for others. Yes, at times life is painful and disappointing but it is also fulfilling and wonderful. Life is to be celebrated!

The founders of the United States interpreted this first inalienable right to life as whatever "living fully" meant to all persons of good will.

During the time of Christ, there were many of Jesus' followers who believed that Jesus should save the country from the Romans. They wanted him to secure freedom from Roman rule and occupation of their country. Christ's purpose was not the political purpose of some of his followers. It is a main reason Jesus was betrayed, especially by Judas. Their desire for freedom from

Rome was not wrong nor unimportant. But the life of Jesus had a higher purpose, to demonstrate eternal life, to love one another and to help people live more abundantly. The purpose of Christianity is not to end abortion.

Tales of Equality

In the following pages several real-life stories are presented where equality is the primary issue.

Except for the author, family members and the well-known philanthropists, Jack and Dollie Galter, names have been changed for privacy purposes.

Stories about inequality involve race, gender, ethnicity, religion, social and income class distinctions, etc. The first two stories deal with the subject of abortion in regard to equality. Women who are forced to carry a child lose their freedom. Men can lose or sacrifice their future if they do not absolutely follow lock step into denouncing abortion.

Tale 1: Nora's Departure

I had just begun my first year at Shimer College and was attending a reception after dinner when Sally, whose room was next to mine in the dormitory, approached me.

"Have you heard about Nora?" she asked. The three of us had been together in our first Humanities class the day before.

"No," I said, remembering the tall, slender, gracious student from a Chicago suburb who had been so enthusiastic about the class. I had hoped we would become good friends.

"She's gone! They sent her home," Sally said. "I heard her dad was really angry."

"Why?" I asked. "What happened?"

"They made her go home. She threw herself down a set of stairs in Metcalf Hall."

"You're kidding! Why did she do that?"

"Nora is pregnant. She was trying to — end it."

"Did she get hurt?" I asked.

"Just sprained her ankle. Not enough to end her pregnancy. I guess she is very upset. Nora didn't want to go home. I feel bad about her having to leave. "

"So do I!" How could Nora have thrown herself down the stairs? "I can't imagine doing something like that." My heart ached for her. She must have been desperate.

"Well, maybe her boyfriend or whoever the father is, will marry her and they'll live happily ever after," Sally said somewhat jokingly.

Happily, ever after? Well, maybe. But as little as I knew her, I realized she was ambitious and had a lot to offer. Nora would make a good life; I had confidence in her, but it wouldn't be the one she had planned. That was gone! I could only wish her well.

I would never hear from her again.

From my Rear View Mirror:

I never heard anything more about Nora, who was not in school long enough to make friends, but I never forgot her. Now I think of Nora because after 50 years, abortion has again become a criminal offense rather than a personal decision, which is going to cause needless deaths and heartbreak, likely for thousands of women in our country.

This is a matter of freedom. One must have control of one's body in order to be free.

Today I send love and blessings to Nora and all the Nora's in our country who along with their families are forced to conform to an ideology which does not honor their principles and beliefs.

Tale 2: The County Commissioner's Swan Song

For many years, my husband and I, along with many friends, attended the Farstrup-Mortensen lecture series in California. *"Atterdag"* had been a folk school in Solvang CA in years past, and attending the lecture series was a treasured way of continuing the Danish folk school tradition of life-long learning.

All the lectures were worth attending. I especially recall a lecture I heard in the early 90's, the last evening of a series on Politics and Religion, when a local County Commissioner spoke at our banquet. Introduced as a well-known, well-liked member of the local community, the vineyard owner presented an unusual message.

He began his talk by thanking us for being there and for the invitation to speak. He confided that if he were running for office again, he would not be making the speech he was about to give. I couldn't help but wonder why a man who was no longer running for public office had been asked to speak. He must be well liked.

"I am an Episcopalian and throughout my adult life I have been a person who is strongly anti-abortion," he said. "But I have always believed it is a personal matter of profound consequences. I do not believe it is the role of government to make abortion illegal. I consider abortion to be highly personal and a matter of faith."

The commissioner explained due to his position on abortion, he would no longer be a candidate for public office. I was amazed to hear that his Republican colleagues would not support his re-election and would even prefer the opposition be elected than their fellow Republican who was a highly valued member of the community. Why did his colleagues prefer to lose an election more than re-elect someone so well liked, whose values were similar to their own? He was clearly anti-abortion! Didn't they consider that better than electing the opposition? It didn't make sense!

The obvious pain the speaker was feeling over what had happened to his political legacy and perhaps also to his political party was palpable. One and only one view would be allowed in the coming election and his modest position on this one subject of abortion apparently outweighed any other matter.

That evening I assumed it was just a limitation of this particular California locality. It did not occur to me that such authoritarian regulation of running for office would become the rule of enforcement in either political party.

I was wrong! They were just a little ahead of what was to become the strategy to create discord, a strategy to begin ending democracy.

From the Rear View Mirror:

Today, 30 some years later I can see what was then my introduction to the intentional absolutism that has been successful in changing the Republican party. It has eliminated the careers of many talented, able Republican politicians and affected all of us. This "one way or the highway" method of operating has ruined the Republican party, eliminating needed ideas and actions which could have major benefits for our country. Similar absolute conformity is active at times within the Democratic party and other organizations, but has not been as obvious or as successful. The purpose of the method is to establish minority rule.

Authoritarianism by definition, is anti-democratic and very dangerous. We are in danger of losing tolerance for diversity, and the great richness it brings to society. If that be the case, and this absolutism is how our government is run in the future, it will no longer be a democracy. The divine experiment will fail if we do not recognize our interdependence and accept essential equality.

The Inalienable Right of Liberty (Freedom)

In the last 10 years, the words freedom and liberty have become linked with the right to own weapons of war. Equating gun ownership with freedom (liberty) has led to a tenfold increase in gun ownership. The powerful NRA has had crushing success in allowing easy purchase of automatic weapons for millions of people and successful opposition to universal registration such as licensing drivers of automobiles. Gun ownership is not a matter of patriotism; but like driving an automobile or flying an airplane, it is a matter of the relationship between an individual and a dangerous machine.

Driving an automobile requires a license. While we have accidents today, think of what would happen if we did not require drivers' licenses! For the common good of all, we want to make certain that a person behind the steering wheel is quite capable of driving and will practice a degree of caution. If we did not have licenses, many more people would die on our highways.

We consider it reasonable to require standards for people to drive automobiles! We restrict smoking in restaurants because it is a health hazard. What about guns?

A person has the right to defend himself. An individual has the right to hunt game in season, but no individual has the right to purchase weapons of mass destruction to use in mass killings of innocent individuals and groups of people.

Weapons of war were never designed for hunting ducks nor for protecting one's life or personal property. They are meant to kill people, to disregard the health and lives of others, including our children. The 2022 tragedy in Robb Elementary School in Texas is appalling. The ability to allow such a travesty was never the intention of the second amendment.

Gun laws established by careless state legislatures have nothing to do with personal freedom. They are dominated by fear, self-indulgence or irresponsible self-interest with disregard for the freedom of others. Such irresponsibility was never the intent of the Declaration of Independence and in total disregard for the Declaration of *Interdependence*.

Historically, the National Rifle Association was an organization concerned with gun safety, and supportive of hunting as a sport. Today, it is a powerful lobby which completely disregards the safety of the most vulnerable. The NRA of today is most concerned with engendering fear, distrust of government, and controlling votes nationwide for self-interest. Their program increases the wealth of a few, and endangers the lives of thousands under the guise of freedom and patriotism.

The innocent people who have been murdered by gun violence had their rights to life taken from them. Liberty, true freedom, is only accomplished when a particular action has equal consideration of its effect on the freedom of others.

The Inalienable Right to Pursue Happiness

What is happiness?

Happiness is the result of helpful, harmonious, enjoyable, loving relationships with other people and fulfilling the purpose of what one feels called to do. It requires compassion, empathy, perception, intentions and expressing one's individual gifts.

What is not happiness? A relentless drive to achieve only self-interest goals with disregard for the common good does not bring happiness to anyone. Conversely, to please everyone else with disregard for oneself is irresponsible and is equally unsuccessful in obtaining happiness.

Sublimating personal happiness in a sacrificial way with a magnified idea of self-importance is mutually disastrous. Whether in disregard for others or in worship of someone else's opinions, ego-driven goals lead to unrequited attempts for fulfillment.

If happiness was the result of having the most stuff, or the greatest financial worth, people who are richest would always be the happiest people in the world and those with less would all be unhappy. It doesn't work that way. Endless pursuit of material goods engenders greed rather than long term happiness, whether one is poor or rich. Quite simply, you can never get enough of what you don't need.

Most advertisements promise happiness and personal fulfillment from obtaining a key acquisition—a particular car, a new refrigerator, the latest make-up, medications, clothing, furniture, etc. Acquiring something new often temporarily increases pleasure, but it is not happiness itself. Happiness cannot be purchased, inherited or stolen.

"The person who dies with the most toys—wins!" is so

ludicrous it is an embarrassment to quote. Many people, by the time of their deaths, no longer care much about their toys at all; they have probably outgrown them, and simply enjoy them as memories.

The pursuit of happiness is an inalienable right! But happiness itself is not an inalienable right. No one is guaranteed happiness. The constitution does not guarantee it! We have the right to seek happiness. Far too many people in the United States and certainly around the world, do not have that opportunity. It is up to us to make our inalienable right to pursue happiness more accessible.

To be happy necessitates basic security— sufficient food, shelter, basic health and safety. Only when these necessities are present, can we co-create the kind of life we choose to have.

How can we assure that opportunities to pursue happiness are available to more people? While a society must not weaken personal motivation by supplying too many personal needs, we have an obligation to provide a safety net of food, shelter, basic health and safety. Once necessities are assured, the next level includes opportunities to become educated, to have a job, a family, contribute to the community, follow one's heart, make dreams come true, and develop one's potential. Often it is the journey itself rather than the goal that yields the most happiness.

Modes to Disparage Equality

Several approaches (modes) can be taken to decrease equality. Disparaging people by labeling them according to their race, ethnicity, gender, financial or social status are "Put Downs," indicating an individual is of lesser worth by negatively and unfairly associating them with an entire group of people.

Most people have experienced unkind remarks or actions about their race, gender, ethnicity or class. We also may have been guilty of making "Put Downs," judging others as inferior by group characteristics. We may act silently, or use words that are hurtful. Unkind actions or hurtful remarks tend to be contagious and spread. We often are not aware of the harm we have done, the unopened doors we have closed, the intentions that would have succeeded, the contributions that would have been made. Such deeds are responsible for the hardening of hearts and minds, and are a setback to recognizing the essential equality of human others. We can do better.

Racism is the most toxic and painful limitation to experiencing equality. My experiences with racism are less severe and less costly than what most others experience. I nevertheless hope each of us can be a catalyst for change, beginning with ourselves.

Tale 3: A Perfect Baby

I became personally acquainted with racism when I became a mother of my adopted daughter. Thea Marie's birth mother is Irish; her biological father, Puerto Rican.

At the time we lived in Chicago and the State of Illinois policy restricted adoptions of children to parents of the same ethnic/racial mix, a requirement which was eventually changed. As a result of the law, when it was in effect, hundreds of babies and children of all ages waited and waited for adoption.

Thea's birth mother was unable to care for her child. Rosie, a college friend, had separated from her family; the baby's father did not even know of the child's birth. Rosie asked if we would adopt her child who was in a Catholic orphanage, a process which could be accomplished while she still had rights to her, which would end when the baby became six months old. John and I had not yet started a family.

After giving the matter of adoption short but deep consideration, we agreed to become parents. One factor was that in my husband's family baby girls were rare. The adoption would provide us with a daughter, and as anticipated in the years ahead that followed, I gave birth to two sons.

We asked a lawyer, a neighbor who lived in our apartment building, to help arrange a private adoption which would be reviewed by the State of Illinois Department of Children and Family services. Neither my husband nor I were Catholic, but the orphanage was overcrowded and ethnically qualified parents were unlikely to apply.

Through a court order I was able to visit the baby in the orphanage. She had been baptized in the orphanage as Mary Jo. A nun brought her to me. A red ribbon was taped to the top of her nearly bald head. Her presence was amazing! The baby was not at all the passive infant we had been told to expect. She seemed to ask why had I kept her waiting!

"She is a perfect baby except for her blood. She'll darken during the summer. I've studied a lot of anthropology," the nun said. Her manner with the baby seemed racist and inappropriate to me.

"If and when you return, bring clothing. She leaves only with a diaper." The nuns were trying to do the best they could with too many babies.

A few days later John and I left the orphanage with our new baby girl having received custody through the courts. As we walked out, I heard one of the nuns say, "Well, at least she's been baptized!"

We named her Thea Marie. Her first name, Thea, is pronounced Tay-ah, after Mayor LaGuardia's first wife from the hit musical we had recently watched at Timberlake Playhouse, the summer theater where my husband and I were actors in the theater's original company. Marie was a family name for girls in my family—including me.

We were given a short sheet of green paper about her schedule and diet. It was restrictive. I suppose the orphanage had budget concerns. According to our instructions she had her last bottle of milk at 4 o'clock in the afternoon and nothing more until 7 o'clock the next morning! Food was measured in tablespoons. I was horrified and afraid of giving her too much to eat or drink for fear she would become ill, but the pediatrician encouraged us to allow her to have as much as she wanted. Gradually, Thea learned to drink without tensing her entire body while taking her bottle.

At first she did not cry. Aware of the huge lack of loving care she had endured for so long, I was the one who one day wept because it felt like I couldn't do enough to make up for what she had missed—being held, walked, rocked, sung to, loved. But in spite of what she had missed, Thea soon began to really blossom!

Fortunately, the pediatrician was incorrect regarding what to expect. Instead of being delayed, her development was early. At 10 months she had an extensive vocabulary and walked! Thea was a beautiful baby, and a delight! She especially loved to be outdoors in her baby buggy or stroller. Our many friends adored her.

But one of my closest friends asked, "She is so beautiful! What are you going to do when you have your own children and they aren't as beautiful as she is?"

I was speechless. Perhaps I should have said, "We'll just keep her in a closet." But of course, I did not!

Thea and I took a train trip at Christmas for her to meet her grandparents. On the train, a woman across the aisle said to me, "She isn't really your baby, is she?"

"Yes, she's really my baby," I said.

"I mean she isn't really your baby!!" she said with a smile, but her eyes were glaring at me.

"Yes," She really is! She really is my baby!" And that was that!

From the Rear View Mirror:

The nun, my friend, and the strange woman on the train are examples of thoughtless unkindness. They seemed to be trying to drive a wedge between me as a mother and my baby. Remarks like that are not helpful!

Forgive and bless! Such unkindness often comes from people who received unkindness themselves and they may be unwarily passing it on. Be compassionate! And when possible, see the humor!

Tale 4: A Last Ride on Chicago's EL

During the hot summer when Thea was two years old, John and I decided to move to Davenport, Iowa where John was recruited to be the chairman of the Humanities Department at St. Katherine/s St Mark's preparatory school. I would teach English courses part time and direct some plays.

The combined boarding and day school had a new headmaster and chaplain, both of whom had been on staff at Shimer College, our alma mater. The Victorian-appearing campus overlooked the Mississippi River; it had an excellent preschool program and was only an hour away from where my parents had retired. It seemed perfect!

After taking a train to see our new home on campus the three of us returned to Chicago with four empty suitcases to repack for the final trip. We loved Chicago; I was nostalgic about leaving the windy city. "Let's ride home on the 'El' (Elevated trains go through virtually all the interesting Chicago neighborhoods.) It was not the most direct route but John humored me and although it was becoming dark, he agreed. So, we took our empty suitcases and carried our young daughter up the inner-city stairs to the El platform and set out for the 55th street stop south of the loop.

There were no two seats together available on the train. I sat on an aisle seat holding Thea, and John sat directly in front of us, also on the aisle. The suitcases were set next to an open space near the doorway.

Behind Thea and I, a heavy set, young black man in his 20s, was sprawled across both seats behind us. When the train began moving, Thea stood up on my lap and looked back at the man behind us.

"Why's that baby looking at me?" he asked angrily.

I pulled her down on my lap. "Sorry," I said. But Thea was fascinated with him and managed to get up and stare at him again, which again upset him.

"Stop her from looking at me!" he insisted, bending toward us. I set her down on my lap and tried to get her attention away from the man behind us, but neither rattling keys nor anything else seemed to work. I wished there was some way I could communicate to him, but there was nothing I could do or say that would have helped.

Thea continued to be fascinated by the strange young man behind us. There was something wrong with him. Unfortunately, I could not get John's attention. I would have given Thea to him, but he had no idea what was going on between the young man and us. He didn't realize I wanted his help.

"I told you to stop her! Stop her from looking at me!"

I covered part of her face with my hand, which she protested. By now I had to admit that going home on the El was not such a great idea. The train jolted on, and we continued on with Thea trying to get a look at the mysterious stranger every chance she had.

A couple of stops later, the train jerked into the station. Before I could think, the young man in back of me jumped up, bent over the back of our seat and grabbed my black purse from under my arm and quickly ran out the train door. Holding Thea, I stood up and screamed, "He's got my purse!"

John, seeing my purse, which had nearly all our cash money, exit out the door in the hands of the man, instantly got up and ran after him, managing to get out the doors just before they slammed shut and the train started up again.

I heard myself wailing over the sound of a group of teenage boys laughing at my predicament.

The train started again and I cried out, "Help! Help!" It was only then that I realized that with John gone, Thea and I were the only ones in the car who were not black. I was frightened, but not as much as I was worried about what might be happening to John. The man he was chasing was probably high or mentally ill, and likely dangerous.

John should not have chased him! I managed to move a couple of suitcases closer to the door; there was no way I could possibly carry a child and four suitcases.

I had to get off at the next stop. John and I had made a pact that if were ever separated on the El, the person remaining on the train should get off at the next stop so we could find each other. (This was long before cell phones.)

When the train stopped, I got off with Thea. Two men picked up our suitcases and took them off the train. At first, I didn't know if they were helping me or stealing the suitcases, but it made no difference; I couldn't handle suitcases, either way. I was very grateful to them. They were helping!

On the platform, the two men set down the suitcases and kindly offered more help, but I needed to wait for John. I thanked them and they left. I was near tears from worry and gratitude. Thea, who seemed shaken, was quiet.

Ten, then fifteen minutes passed. A train stopped, but John did not get off. Then another. I was very worried, but did not allow myself to think about what I could or should do. I knew John was not equipped to handle the man he had chased. All I could do was wait. And hope.

Another train. Then, almost to my disbelief, John, looking

worn and anxious but otherwise okay, was coming out the train door! All six feet six inches of him! He gave me a quick hug and kissed Thea on the forehead. I was relieved he was okay, but obviously exhausted and shaken.

"What happened?" I asked.

He reached under his jacket and produced a butcher knife with a six-inch blade. "I chased him down the stairs from the platform. He was waiting for me at a corner on the stairs. He had thrown the purse on the floor. I picked it up, just like he intended. He pulled the knife on me, but was so drunk or high that in the process he dropped the knife and fell backward down the stairs. I picked up the knife, ran back and got on the next train as fast as I could."

"Thank God!" I said. I stared at the big ugly knife that had been meant for his stomach or chest; I opened my purse.

Nothing was inside. No money. My billfold was missing and John didn't have enough cash on him to pay for a cab.

We got back on the train until we arrived at our intended station. After talking with police and showing them the knife, they reluctantly agreed to drive us to our apartment in Hyde Park.

I was getting Thea ready for bed when she finally spoke after being so very quiet. "My tummy hurts." For several months after the El ride home, Thea, whenever under stress, would say, "My tummy hurts."

I held her tightly as we said prayers. How much we had to be thankful for!

From the Rear View Mirror:

When I look back on this incident, I feel myself staring at the young man like my daughter had stared at him. Why are you so angry? How did you become so lost, in such distress? The young man's misbehavior has nothing to do with the shade of his skin. Some decades earlier it likely could have been someone from another minority that had turned to petty crime in order to survive.

The legacy of slavery in America, the practice of prejudice based on skin color, the evils of slave "ownership," the failures of reconstruction and pain of integration has made change difficult---so much to admit to, so much to forgive, so much to change.

I do not believe racism is unsolvable. There is much to be gained by rejecting racism. We can improve education, increase availability of opportunities, and insist on equal justice. We can bring about real change! The young man who sat behind Thea and I that day was once a potential resource for greater goodness, someone who could have contributed more to society. His life could have been different! Our last El ride might have been very different. Thea was not judging him. We should not judge him harshly.

Tale 5: The Teacher

In 1978 I got a divorce, and moved with my three children to Wisconsin to work for the Greater Milwaukee United Way, a four-county area. After living in a downtown hotel for a couple of months, we moved before school started to a modern condominium on the far northwest corner of the city. My youngest child, Noah, was in third grade.

When I first met Noah's teacher at the school named Happy Hill, she seemed unfriendly, not like the teachers where my children had previously attended. I shared concerns about my son Noah having trouble learning to read. (It was not until years later that we learned he had dyslexia.) A black teacher in a white community, the teacher was uneasy and seemed to lack self confidence. I was expecting to be reassured. Perhaps this was her first year of teaching or working at Happy Hill, which explained her lack of self confidence. Integration was still new in Milwaukee.

A few weeks later, I talked to Noah's teacher over the telephone about Noah not bringing home his papers from school. She told me she didn't have time to send papers home with students, and anyway, Noah was a crybaby, which I couldn't imagine. When asked why he had cried she said it was because he had forgotten his lunch money and didn't get anything for lunch that day, which I did not know. I would have cried too if I were hungry and in a new school, but I didn't say so.

Noah's grades went from bad to worse. I continued to not receive his work assignments or samples of what he was doing at school. Finally, I requested a conference. A meeting was set up with the teacher, the principal, a school psychologist and another teacher.

At first it was not going well. The psychologist pointed out that Noah was from a "broken home" and we were new in the community.

Finally, giving up, I asked the teacher if she would just, please send Noah's papers home with corrections so I could help him. To my surprise, the teacher refused, "I have other children in class who need a lot more help than he does," she said.

Immediately, the tone of the group changed; the principal, psychologist and other teacher immediately agreed that Noah should transfer to a charter school which had a reading lab. They would arrange for him to go by taxi each morning (without charge) and even start the following Monday!

Noah began attending an integrated inner city charter school with a special reading program. The rest of the year was academically uneventful. I was amazed and thankful!

In the Rear View Mirror:

Looking back, I realize that maybe the teacher actually did have several children who needed help at least as much or more than Noah! She may have been overwhelmed. This all happened during the early years of school integration in Milwaukee! Integration was and is necessary! However, it can be difficult for children, families, and teachers.

Was this Noah's teacher's first teaching job? New to the school? She needed help and may have had few resources she could trust. I am glad that Noah was transferred from Happy Hill. His difficulty reading needed attention, and it was not a supportive environment for him.

Due to dyslexia, my son continued to have challenges but he learned how to compensate for his difficulties. Noah graduated from the University of Illinois with special honors in economics. Years later he received a second degree in spiritual psychology from the University of California, Santa Monica.

Tale 6: My Daughter's Friends

Our first year living in Milwaukee was Thea's last year in Junior High. She had spent the summer in Hawaii with her aunt, uncle and cousins, and it was quite an adjustment to come back to the mainland.

Most mornings, I drove her to school. Soon she was asking me to drop her off a block from the entrance and at first, I did so, but then I asked her why.

"My friends don't like white mothers," she explained. I was stunned by the realization of how difficult our move to Milwaukee was for my daughter. "Sorry to hear that," I said, and drove right to the front entrance of the school.

Now, in retrospect, I wish we had talked about it, but frankly I didn't know what to say.

From the Rear View Mirror:

It is likely that Thea's friends were taught for good reasons by their parents and/or friends to distrust white mothers. Sometimes it is preferable to be the first to reject someone before you get rejected.

Now I wish I had done more to get to know her friends and for them to get to know me. Her friends did not live close to us. How difficult it must have been for my daughter!

Tale 7: Robert, BWD

Shortly after beginning my new job at United Way of Greater Milwaukee, I was given an extra assignment, supervising a housing program; the director reported to me. It turned out Robert was a talented, handsome young man, who needed little supervision and did an excellent job.

Then one day I asked if he could stay late and to my surprise, he said he couldn't, because he did not drive home in the dark. I didn't understand. I could not believe that this able man was worried about driving home in the dark! (I had not yet heard of BWD, Black While Driving.)

A few weeks later the blood-soaked swollen face of a black man's photo, thankfully not Robert, was displayed on the TV news and in the newspapers. After being stopped by police on the freeway for a minor infraction, the man was hospitalized, nearly beaten to death.

I cannot count the number of questionable police beatings and killings of young black men that have been published or shown on TV since then. When I began writing this book, the police murder of George Floyd and subsequent killing of Rayshard Brooks were the latest questionable killings that involved police brutality. The country seemed to recognize these cases demanded we take a stand. To tolerate the inhumanity in such incidents and not insist on accountabilities is to consciously support injustice; it allows and encourages society to become more inhumane which is unfair to the many responsible policemen who act humanely.

Albuquerque and other cities are having difficulty recruiting and hiring policemen. It is a potentially very dangerous job which requires intelligence, physical ability, honesty and strength of character. It is a controversial position which can become very public.

Federal oversight, body cameras and increased awareness have opened the public's eye to the number and depth of injustices which occur. In some cities police brutality and white supremacy has finally been unmasked. We must now find ways to resolve the situation. It is important to appreciate and honor those police and other public servants who provide us with needed and difficult services but insist on accountability for those who harm our fellow citizens.

From the Rear View Mirror:

Police unions have enabled some police to take advantage by providing immunity from liability. There is a valid reason for having some protection, but unfortunately, for some police, liability protection has become an insurance policy which keeps them from being held accountable. We must guarantee justice for everyone, including the police. Immunity from accountability must not be allowed for any job or guaranteed by any union.

As I write this, it is more than two years since the deaths of George Floyd and Rayshard Brooks. The man sentenced for 22.5 years, Derek Chauvia, has filed grievances challenging the George Floyd decision and is requesting an appeal. Garrett Rolfe, who shot Rayshard Brooks and who was fired, then reinstated with back pay, later put on leave. He faced criminal charges but was also cleared of "wrongdoing." Derek was suing the city of Atlanta. Will this never end? It seems like these cases go on forever with accountability being constantly challenged.

We need to ensure justice! Not just for victims; not for just police, but for all. Racism is endemic in the United States; it infects and affects every single person, every community. There is no escape from it. The root of racism is fear, the opposite of love, compassion and empathy. We can only achieve justice through fairness, facts, and objectivity. We need the police. We need order!

I depend on fair and caring policemen. I need them—and not just for myself. I need them for everyone! I need police who would help the young man who sat in the seat back of me on the train, if he were injured in his fall down the El stairs and needed help. I need the police to be kind to Noah's teacher, if she is robbed or has a car accident. I need the police to help Robert if someone attacks him on his way home. I need policemen to help make life better for everyone who needs it—everyone with whom I interact—and with those with whom I don't.

Tale 8: Anna's Manners

In my senior year at Shimer College, I had a new roommate named Anna. We got along very well. Anna had an unusual graciousness about her, perhaps because she had grown up in a formal environment in India, where her father was a diplomat and the family did a lot of formal entertaining.

She was always polite. Anna had a presence unlike anyone else I knew.

The first holiday vacation of the school year came at Thanksgiving. Anna was pleased about going to Chicago to meet her boyfriend's family. She and Kirk had been dating since school started, and seemed very much in love.

Our first evening back at school, Anna asked me for an opinion. She was a private person. We had not talked much since we returned. Anna was sitting at her desk, with pen in hand, apparently writing a note.

"How was your visit?" I asked. "Did you like Kirk's parents? How did it go?"

"It was not what I expected. We came back early."

"Early? Why was that?" I asked.

"Well," Anna said, "We got there late Wednesday night. The maid met us and took us directly to the kitchen because we hadn't had dinner. She took some beef stroganoff leftovers from one of the refrigerators. It was quite good. Kirk was upset that his parents didn't come in and say hello to us. He asked the maid where they were, but she said she didn't know. Then, after a while, Kirk's sister Irene came in. She's younger than Kirk—a senior in prep school."

"It doesn't sound like much of a welcome," I said.

"His sister wouldn't look at me," Anna continued. "She spoke directly to Kirk, told him that we would have to leave in the morning. Their parents didn't want to meet me."

"What? After driving all that way? Didn't they expect you?"

"I think so. Kirk told me they knew I was coming. His sister said, 'Mother says she doesn't want her grandchildren to have big noses.'"

Anna was an elegant Jewish woman with a beautiful profile.

"That's horrible! I can't believe someone would say anything like that. That's crazy! "

"It was rather disappointing. Kirk was really upset. He marched right out of the kitchen with Irene following him. The maid left too. I stayed in the kitchen and could hear Kirk almost yelling. I suppose he was talking with his father and mother. It wasn't going well, but I couldn't hear their words."

"That's probably just as well!"

"Anyway, Kirk came back. He was so upset. He opened up a bottle of wine and we had a couple of drinks and talked for a while."

"What did Kirk say?"

"Just that he was so sorry. He said his parents were idiots and they embarrassed him. That I shouldn't pay any attention to them. He was ashamed of them."

"So, what did you do?"

"We went upstairs. They live in a mansion. I had a very nice room and could look out at a garden which was lovely, even in the dark. The next morning, Kirk knocked on my door. It was early, but

Kirk had already eaten. I got dressed and went downstairs. I wasn't hungry so we each had a cup of coffee and then we left."

"You left? You didn't even have breakfast?"

"No. We left. We came back here."

"You didn't have Thanksgiving dinner with his family?"

"No. We just came back and ate in the local restaurant downtown. They were serving turkey dinners with cranberry sauce."

"What about you and Kirk?"

"I don't know. Kirk is angry with them. He says not to pay any attention to them. But they are his parents. I don't see how it can work out for us, but we'll see."

"I'm so sorry," I said.

"They just don't know better," Anna said. "Poor Kirk."

"Yes, I feel bad for him."

"They are pathetic!" I said.

"Yes, it is too bad. I am trying to write to them, and I… "

"You are writing to them? What about?"

Anna looked at me, and shrugged. "Thanking them. It's a thank you note. I'd like your advice."

I couldn't believe it.

"You're writing a thank you note? WHY?"

"Well, I did have dinner there, and stayed overnight. I would not have liked driving back that night. I always write thank-you notes when I have been a guest, but I am worried they might think—well that I'm making fun of them, and that's not the case.

I feel sorry for them and sad for Kirk. I did appreciate staying there for a night."

I looked at Anna. She was not kidding. "You do as you wish, Anna. But I would not send them a thank you note."

"You wouldn't?"

"No, I would not."

From the Rear View Mirror:

Anna was something else.

I admire her graciousness. I think she was right if she went ahead with the thank you note. I would not have done it, because I could not honestly thank them. Perhaps it would be unkind to send them a sympathy note for having lost the respect of their son and missing the opportunity to have such a wonderful daughter-in-law.

Irene. She's the one for whom I feel the most compassion. She seems dependent on copying her mother's ways without even thinking about it. She carelessly, mindlessly, repeats unpleasant slurs and isn't at all aware of her family's limitations.

Irene is unable to recognize the pain and distrust she is causing her brother, who could use her support. She is unable to sense Ann's abilities, and acknowledge the beauty of the woman whom her brother loves. She treats Anna shamefully, Anna who might have become a good friend or even like a sister to her!

Send Irene blessings! And Anna and Kirk too!

Tale 9: Girl or Boy?

I was born as a replacement child for my brother Paul who died tragically at only two months of age from a heart defect. My parents were left handling deep grief, especially my mother. I seem to have known from the beginning that my purpose in life was to cheer up my mother. I have a memory, although implausible, that my mother's first response when she looked at me, was "It's not Paul."

However, they did name me "Joy." My father said they gave me that name because when the doctor spanked my bottom, instead of crying, I laughed. This I very much doubt.

The grief over Paul's short life made me feel I had to succeed, do especially well, be as good or better than boys because of their tragic loss. I mention this because I do not think most parents are aware of what "replacement" children might perceive in such situations.

From my early childhood I realized that boys were more important than girls. If only I were a boy, I could do the "fun" things like play football and real basketball. (It was then against South Dakota law for girls to run full court.)

I was quite good at sports. At the junior high Turner County track meet, I received blue or sometimes red ribbons in the 100-yard dash, running broad jump, and jumping rope (we had rope-jumping contests), standing broad jump and high jumping. When I was in 7th grade, I was drafted to run in the four-person relay which was meant for boys, but Viborg Junior High was short of boys in that particular age group, especially boys who could run fast. Because I was the fourth fastest 7th grader, I was chosen to run with three boys. My delight over being chosen to run with the boys turned into an embarrassment when our team came in 4th. I heard our team captain say, "We would have won if it wasn't for her." What bothered me most was that he was right.

Almost always when we visited relatives or friends there would be questions about my brother David—what was he doing in school? Did he play basketball? Football? What were his plans? Such questions were seldom asked of me or my sister. This may have had something to do with familial relationships. It was different from my uncle on my mother's side, who had more interest in my sister and I, but conversation concerning girl offspring was more about which one of us was more attractive.

When I was in junior high my Uncle Leif gave me a clarinet, and said, "This is a good instrument for a girl." As a result, although I played clarinet in the school band, I never really liked it, and in high school happily traded it in for a tenor sax. (Since then, I have learned about Benny Goodman and now have a musical grandson who loves to play the clarinet.)

My uncle was a trumpet player and traveled with a big band for a decade before going into the advertising business. My sister chose a trumpet and played first trumpet in our high school band. To be fair, Uncle Leif always treated me respectfully. He showed great love, respect and even awe for his mother (my grandmother.) However, his view of women reflected his time and status in the community. Women should be very pretty, support their husband in every facet of life, take care of the children, and not stick out too much, or embarrass them. This was typical of the ideal woman well into the 1960s.

As a teenager, I did not want to become a woman; and did not especially want to have children, although I assumed it was something I would have to do.

I woke the morning of the school's 7th-8th grade picnic, with a very sore throat. I could tell I had the mumps. And then I got up and looked in the mirror and saw that in addition to two big lumps in my neck, my entire body was broken out in red spots. I had both measles and mumps at the same time. To top that off, I was bleeding—I had become a woman. Some picnic!

When I was in college a woman's career was considered secondary to any man's. Career choices for women were mostly limited to teaching, nursing, secretarial work or waitressing. Of course, there were exceptions. When I was in graduate school at University of Chicago Divinity School one of the few women students at the time received a PhD and went to teach at a college with her husband—for half salary.

No one including my family took my pursuit of Religion and Literature seriously. The Divinity School had only one small restroom for the few women who were there. Today, more than half of student bodies for religious studies or in seminary are female. I am so glad!

From the Rear View Mirror:

Gradually, I learned to like being female and I am now happy with my gender. There are advantages and disadvantages in whichever gender you are. The women's movement came just in time for me. It became apparent that I needed to make a living to support my family.

It is no longer unusual for the woman to be the household's prime wage earner and for the man to be the prime caregiver and homemaker. Generally, whatever the arrangement, men do significantly more caregiving and women have more financial responsibilities than their parents ever had. Same sex couples, like everyone else, divide household responsibilities according to personal abilities and wishes.

Thankfully, today there is now more equality in expectations and in household roles regardless of gender; this is likely to result in couples enjoying greater equality, interdependence—and independence.

We are all interdependent.

I have witnessed evidence of love between races in the Black Lives Matter movement. Overcoming racism is about finding the common good in all human beings and loving humanity enough to insist on accountability. This is about evolution.

Gender and Homosexuality

A leveling of gender expectations in society has helped pave the way for acceptance of homosexuality. For a child to have two mothers or two fathers instead of one of each was unthinkable when I was a young adult. Now it is not uncommon. In the last 30 years society has made fantastic strides in accepting gender changes and changes in gender. This rapid change has been difficult for some people to accept, but most people recognize that every person has both masculine and feminine traits.

A gay friend of mine pointed out to me that the term is itself troublesome because it implies homosexual relationships are primarily if not exclusively sexual. Both heterosexual and homosexual relationships have emotional, social, mental, and spiritual qualities.

A 2021 Pew Research Center survey finds that 5.1% of adults younger than 30 are trans or nonbinary, including 2.0% who are a trans man or trans woman and 3.0% who are nonbinary – neither a man nor a woman or aren't strictly one or the other. This compares with 1.6% of 30- to 49-year-olds and 0.3% of those 50 and older who are trans or nonbinary. Obviously, the older generation has had different experiences when it comes to gender issues.

Since April 2022, Americans have been allowed to choose an X for gender on their passport applications and select their sex on Social Security cards. This June the State Department said U.S. citizens could select their gender on applications without having to submit medical documentation. Nonbinary, intersex and gender-nonconforming people now have an option other than male or female on their travel documents.

Tale 10: The Screen

When I arrived to work for The United Way of Greater Milwaukee, I learned that a staff member had left and the annual campaign was going to begin in a few months. I was assigned to raise $2 million dollars from some of Milwaukee's larger companies including Coca-Cola and Harley-Davidson. In a few weeks twenty loaned executives would report to me to train and help raise the funds.

I was unfamiliar with Milwaukee and had never raised money in a campaign. I tried to convince them that I was inexperienced. My work had always been in government relations, proposal writing and obtaining grants.

I could not quit my job. Our house had been sold. I had to make this new job work. For the first week, when the kids were not with me, I cried driving to and from work, but by the second week I started liking my new job. After the 20 executives showed up, I really enjoyed it.

My new boss asked me to serve as planner for the entire campaign since I had worked as a planner for Model Cities. This meant attending a meeting each Monday morning with the President, the Vice President of United Way and the volunteer Chairman of the current year's campaign. We would set and review goals and strategies, and bring in other people as needed throughout the campaign. We met at a private Milwaukee club close to our office, the club of Milwaukee's "doers and shakers".

Monday mornings had to be well planned. I had to be out of the house by 7:00 am. The kids had to be awake, breakfast food and bowls on the table, agreement on what the boys were going to wear, and clarity on the books, money, and papers they needed to bring to school.

The first Monday morning, as we entered the dining area, the president, Dan, said, "Sorry about that screen," as we passed a nondescript Japanese screen on the way to our table. As we walked on, I noticed a number of tables on the other side of the screen but did not question why we went on to a smaller room directly ahead.

My boss was particularly fussy about quality and appearances, so I had accepted his criticism of the screen. On my first day at work, he had called me in and insisted I always wear suits and hose. Accustomed to a more relaxed dress code in the Iowa-Illinois quad cities, I was slightly embarrassed when he made such a demand. Being particular about appearance isn't the worst fault in a boss; I accepted his request as well- meaning, although an unexpected expense. I purchased two all-weather suits, and wore them constantly. It turned out to be practical and time saving,

A few Monday mornings later, Dan was unable to be present and Peter, the volunteer Campaign President of the campaign and president of Northwestern Mutual Life escorted me to what had become our table.

Peter said, "I apologize for the screen. I am not in agreement with it."

"What's the problem?" I asked.

"You don't know? It separates those of us who have women with us from the other diners. This is an historic club. There was formerly a separate entrance for women."

"Really! What's the reason do they give?" I asked.

Peter tried to laugh it off. "Well, some say men can't keep their minds on business if women are with them."

"Oh," I said. Fortunately, Bill, our VP, was at the table waiting for us. We sat down and exchanged good mornings. The waiter promptly served us coffee. I took a sip and looked around. I was quiet but I felt resentment. Hadn't I prepared for this meeting? Hadn't I gotten up early, put on a suit, left my children at home to manage without me? Didn't I have everything ready and wasn't I on time? I was doing as much as a man would do, maybe more, in this job!

I was embarrassed that I had walked past the screen numerous times, been treated as a "lesser than" person without realizing it. I felt uncomfortable that the men with me had to dine on this "lesser than" side of the screen because of me. More than anything I wanted to get up and leave. I could visualize going over and knocking the damn screen down.

What would happen if I did? It would hit the Milwaukee Journal--- and ....and ...and I would lose my job.

I did not knock down the screen. Instead, I reminded myself, I need this job. It is a good job. I am fortunate to have it. My children need me to be sane.

After a few minutes I relaxed and was able to contribute to the meeting. The men with me were not the cause of the inequity. No reason to embarrass and trouble them.

Sometimes a person has to take what's dealt and not whimper. On my way out that morning, I stopped in the pink powder room next to the marble staircase near what was once the women's entrance. The club had the most beautiful powder room I have ever been in.

From the Rear View Mirror.

I hope the screen is no longer in the club. I hope the club has taken it down. The screen's antiquated message of inequality is out of place.

While women have more opportunity now for jobs, their

salaries are not yet equal. In 2021 women working full time in the U.S. were still paid 83 cents compared to every dollar earned by men — and it is less for non-white women. Compared to the median weekly earnings of White men working full-time, Hispanic women's full-time earnings were just 58.4 percent, Black women's 63.1 percent, and White women's 79.6 percent. While there have been considerable salary increases for women since 1960, the increases seem to have stalled the last 10 years.

Consequences of this income gap affect women into retirement. (US Bureau of Labor Statistics and The Gender Wage Gap by Occupation, Race, and Ethnicity 2020, Institute for Women's Policy Research.)

Tale 11: The Family Secret

Before I moved away from Chicago, I telephoned my cousin Bob. He and his sister Karen Sue, the children of my Uncle Leif, were the only first cousins I had in the United States. We were never close although I stayed with them for two summers during my college years, working for my uncle at his advertising agency.

Bob was two years younger than I and a champion water skier. When young, Bob skied and ski-jumped all summer. He was a good-looking football player, and talented in almost every sport. His father was not athletic, except for playing golf. My very musical Uncle Leif played his trumpet professionally in big bands for many years before becoming a businessman. Bob and Karen Sue were adopted children. When I spent summers with them my uncle would often compare his children unfavorably to me, for such crimes as my reading books and going to the library. Why didn't they read more like I did? Such comparisons did not help a cousinly relationship.

I liked Bob. He was known to have a temper but he was very down-to-earth and tried his darnedest to please his dad. When Bob married, we went to the wedding and during the early years of their marriage I met their four sons. Once, grown up and "on our own," we saw little of each other. According to what I had heard, Bob's wife had a chronic illness and Bob did most of the parenting.

Before we moved from Chicago, I contacted Bob, whose middle name was "Jens" after my grandfather. I had several diaries that belonged to Jens. Bob was eager to have something tangible that had belonged to our grandfather who had kept diaries for most of his 92 years and I was happy to share them!

I brought Bob three or four of the diaries when we met at a favorite Italian restaurant for lunch. Bob was excited but somewhat disappointed because Jens's diaries, while full of details about each day's weather, visitors, and holidays, reveal little about life. Nothing in Jens' beautifully scripted handwriting indicates how he felt about anything or anyone. Nevertheless, Bob found the diaries interesting. They were like captain logs on a small ship sailing through life via third street in Clinton, Iowa.

Bob shared with me some of his efforts to learn about his adoption, and talked proudly about his four sons; each of them. He was especially proud of the son who was mildly handicapped and worked in a school as a maintenance man. I admired Bob's frankness. "I have been lucky in life, but unlucky in marriage." He didn't go into the details, and I didn't ask. "But I have a good job, and I have four wonderful boys."

It was the only time I ever felt close to my cousin Bob. In addition to our kids we talked about our parents and our grandparents. My grandmother Marie ran the house, but the basement belonged to Jens. A huge octopus furnace occupied the middle of the large basement room and on rainy days we would roller skate around it, passing by the washing machine and laundry tubs.

Jens built beautiful furniture in his basement workshop, and used his printing press to make monogrammed stationery for us kids as well as for our parents. He also had a room where he kept a bottle of whiskey amid shelves of canned goods.

Bob and I enjoyed a glass or two of wine with our delicious lunch. And then Bob told me this story:

"On the morning of my wedding, my dad took me down to the storage room off our family room to talk." In my mind, I followed Bob and Uncle Leif down the stairs of the Juhl's ultra-modern split-level home with a view of the river, into the storage room they once considered making into a bomb shelter. It was the same room I used as a closet when I lived with them.

I also envisioned my grandfather's special dimly lit room with shelves of canned goods and miscellaneous tools, where he and my uncle went that morning. I was familiar with this special room where he shared special moments with his friends because we sometimes hid in there when playing hide and seek. I could see my grandfather pouring a small glass of whiskey in his man's cave and looking directly into my uncle's young musician eyes. His son was about to marry my Aunt Esther; they had been sweethearts since grade school.

I was excited because I was going to learn something from the past that I never knew—wisdom from my uncle and my grandfather and maybe even generations before them.

Bob looked at me intently, speaking slowly. "Dad poured me some whiskey and he told me what he said his dad had told him and what I am going to tell you."

"What did he tell you?" I asked, breathless with anticipation. Bob looked at me, was silent for a moment, and then he answered. "They aren't people."

"What?" I asked, startled.

"They aren't people." Bob repeated.

"They aren't people?" I couldn't believe what I heard! And then I... I .... I started to laugh. It was so ridiculous—so wrong, and yet — so right on! — so perfect!

That was the message Bob had to share with me?

For a moment I suddenly felt doubtful. Could this be nothing more than a usual expression of the difference between women and men; women are intuitive and creative; men are rational. If so, it was a disappointment. I suppose it is possible, but no, my grandfather was creative! He didn't bother with platitudes; he didn't say unimportant things. He would keep quiet rather than say something everyone knew. He was trying to express something momentous—historic—a truth! What did he mean that my grandmother was not people? What was so special and important that he felt was necessary to share with his son?

My grandfather Jens was in awe of my grandmother. When you live with someone for a long time, you discover what a person really is. For Jens, Marie was more than he expected. Marie was much more than just a people.

Living and loving Marie had enriched his life in so many ways. She made each day enjoyable and meaningful. Her wisdom and insights, her compassion was always more than expected. Her way with animals was amazing. He loved the delicious kale soup she made and the beautiful sweaters she knit. The way she sometimes predicted something was going to happen—and then it happened—fascinated him. But he knew she was also a human being and had her faults

Marie went to board meetings and spent a lot of time on the telephone talking about projects and making decisions. She seemed always to have a positive perspective. Jens loved to see how his wife encouraged everyone who needed it—children and adults and how beautifully they responded to her encouragement!

Yes, Marie was more than people. She had something special inside her! Apparently, my grandfather didn't have the words to describe what he perceived in his wife. She had a spark from heaven within her. He might not have been aware of that spark in himself, but he knew there was something incredibly wonderous in his wife.

We have divinity, God, within us. Jens had probably run across this in others, but not as much as he was aware of it in Marie. He had seen snatches of the divine spark in teachers he had helped or fellow workers, and some of the children he befriended.

Human Beings are amazing. We have souls. We're more than just people. We are not man-made machines. Divinity is inherent in every person, man or woman. Sometimes it is dormant, unrealized or undeveloped, but at other times, it shines brightly!

My grandfather wanted his son to be ready to be aware, prepared for living every day with someone who likely also was not a people!

From the Rear View Mirror:

All of us are more than people. To be fully human is to be divine.

Often when I meet someone I think of the Hindu greeting, "Namaste" (nah-ma-stay). Literally, it means 'I bow to you." It is a customary greeting which honors the divine in the other person. It is often used to express more: "The Divine Light in me honors the Divine light in you. We are one." Or "My soul recognizes your soul. I honor the light, love, beauty, truth and kindness within you because it is also in me."

In finding the divine in each other, we acknowledge the divine light in ourselves.

Tale 12: The Church President Confesses

I retired early to go to Michigan's Upper Peninsula to have time to write and "do music." We bought an inexpensive Victorian house built in 1908 in Trout Creek, MI, which has a population hovering around 200. Several friends had moved to the community (increasing the population by about 10%) to escape life in Chicago. I began giving piano lessons and became the organist for Trinity Lutheran Church, less than two blocks away. The clergyman at the church, Pastor Anderson and his wife had moved from Canada to the Trout Creek area to be near their daughter. We became close friends. During the dozen years we lived there, the ELCA (Evangelical Lutheran Church of America) decided to take up the issue of sexuality. Each congregation was to have a discussion-study group, and make a recommendation regarding the church's social statement about homosexuality in preparation for adoption at the 2009 ELCA Churchwide Assembly.

A half dozen of us from the congregation met one evening around two tables set together in the church vestibule. Tall and lean, always courteous Rev. Anderson, opened by reading two familiar passages from the Bible: "Genesis 1: V27: So, God created man in his own image, in the image of God he created him, male and female he created them. And God blessed them...

"Matthew 22:37: And he said to him, 'You shall love the Lord your God with all your heart and with all your soul and with all your mind. This is the great and first commandment. And a second is like it, you shall love your neighbor as yourself.' On these two commandments depend all the law and the prophets."

Anderson suggested that we begin by each of us sharing our thoughts and feelings about homosexuality. Starting us off, Anderson, who was close to retirement age, had moved to the area from Canada. He said his feelings had changed significantly while in Canada. He had counseled two clergymen who were homosexuals; both were married to women who accepted their situations. To his surprise the marriages seemed to work out well for the couples.

Because I was sitting next to Anderson, my turn was next. I talked about my best friend from high school, who went to a Baptist college, where she met and then married a man who became a Baptist minister. Their first child, a son, was gay, which was against the beliefs and policies of their church. Jane and her husband, Steve, had to make a choice between their son, and their church which was also their livelihood.

Fortunately, they chose their son, Lou, and have ever since have centered their lives on furthering the cause of gay rights. They are determined, dedicated activists who enjoy a close relationship with their son who was a diplomat for the State Department and has lived in several countries. They were able to visit him frequently around the world and warmly accepted his Vietnamese husband. It has been a real growth experience for all of the family including their daughter Mary who has attended ashrams in India, influenced by her brother-in-law.

I admire them for their ability to change and adapt, and for all the good their son and the family has accomplished.

Priscilla was next in the circle. She was obviously very nervous. She held a Bible in her right hand and spoke with much emotion, "I'm sorry, but it's wrong!! It is just plain wrong and not what God intends. It says so in the Bible. We need to listen to the Bible, not just our friends! It is not natural. God created us male and female! We need to keep it that way. I do not respect church members who think it is okay, because it is not okay! It is wrong. The church needs to take a stand! What will be next?"

We nodded. Pastor Anderson thanked Priscilla for expressing her feelings so clearly.

THE DECLARATION OF INTERDEPENDENCE

Albert was next. I expected him to sympathize with Priscilla. An older man, still grieving from his wife's death a few months earlier, his comments were very short. "I don't want to talk about it." he said.

"We'd like to hear what you think..." Pastor Anderson said.

"I don't have anything to say. I don't want to talk about it."

"You're sure?"

Albert nodded. "I just don't want to talk about it," he muttered.

Only one person in our small group had not yet spoken—Jim, the president of the congregation who several years ago had returned to Trout Creek, where he grew up. Jim, one of the community's own, had a fine singing voice and was much more popular than those of us who came from cities and had not been born in the Upper Peninsula.

It was now Jim's turn. He sighed, then began speaking with great emotion, saying "Now that my mother's dead"....when we were suddenly interrupted by a latecomer, another "newbie" in the community, named Ted who was a co-owner of a small restaurant in town. "I'm sorry to be late. Had to help clean up the kitchen," Ted explained.

"Sit down," Pastor Anderson said "We have been going around the table saying how we felt about the issue before us."

We all turned back to Jim who was obviously tearful. Ted was now embarrassed, realizing he had interrupted us.

"Now that, Mom has gone," Jim managed, "...I....I want to come out. I want to let you know...know that I am gay."

An audible sound of sighs or simply breathing filled the room. Gay? The walls seemed to argue this new reality. Not Jim, with his fine singing voice, not Jim who sings for every special and many not so special church occasions. Jim...Gay? Jim...the president of the church, gay?

I was surprised by his admission, because I had never seen Jim with a male companion. Jim seemed to prefer the company of women. Now that his mother is gone? I had lived in the community for eight years and his mother died before I came. Why had he waited so long? He had missed so much by not "coming out" sooner!

Priscilla spoke first and her tears matched Jim's. "Oh, Jim! I didn't mean you, Jim! I didn't mean you! Please know, I didn't mean you!" The tears were infectious; I was holding back my own tears.

Jim nodded, "I know, Priscilla, I know. But it's time, now that I have returned to this community, and am president of the church. Well, it's time."

"Congratulations, Jim." I said, "Thank you for telling us."

"Yes," Pastor Anderson. "We're glad you told us. No one loves you any less."

"It is no problem for me." Ted said, "I'm sure that wasn't easy for you."

Albert didn't say anything.

Priscilla was still distressed. "You know I didn't mean you, Jim. Please know, I didn't mean you."

Jim's coming out of the closet was the highlight and end of our deliberations that evening. We sat silently for a moment until Pastor Anderson closed with a prayer.

Later that year, the 2009 Assembly of the ELCA passed a statement which set the way for officially welcoming homosexuals to the Evangelical Lutheran Church of America.

From the Rear View Mirror:

What Priscilla said so poignantly at the meeting that evening should be the mantra for the gay movement. "I don't mean you, Jim! I don't mean you!"

When it comes to prejudice, we do not mean to hurt people we love. We depend on each other and we depend on others to be kind to those we care about. Let's care about everyone more!

It was necessary that churches and other organizations examine their attitudes toward membership and ordination in regard to people who are non-heterosexual. This is new in the history of churches. Only 50 years ago, homosexuality was rarely discussed or recognized. Now LGBTQ is often a family matter. The number of LGBTQ young people is increasing.

As the youngest Americans slowly outnumber and replace the oldest, Gallup predicts the number of LGBTQ-identifying adults will only increase — and at a much faster rate than past generations. The percent of U.S. adults who identify as something other than heterosexual has doubled over the last 10 years, from 3.5 percent in 2012 to 7.1 percent, according to a Gallup poll released in February 2022.

A recent poll showed 59% of LGBTQ had experienced prejudice during the last year (2020). But while prejudice continues, there is a positive development—there is more acceptance as numbers increase! In a November 2021 poll, 81 % of non-LGBTQ Americans indicate they have become more understanding and accepting of the LGBTQ community.

Tale 13: What Not to Give Away

In 1982 we moved to the Chicago area where I began a new job as the Director of Development for Mount Sinai Hospital. Mortgage rates had hit 17%. Selling our condo in Milwaukee and buying a place to live was very difficult. My daughter was now in her first year of college and I moved to Illinois with my two sons. We managed to squeeze into a two-bedroom condominium in the historic district of Oak Park, Illinois.

After a few months, it came time for me to hire a secretary for the Development Office. According to the human resources department someone very skillful but "different" had applied for a secretarial job.

I liked Ronnie as soon as I met him and was happy to hire him. He was handsome, young, and new to Chicago, having just moved from Indiana. He seemed to love the windy city. Leaving Indiana apparently had been painful. Later, I learned his father had disowned him because he was gay.

Ronnie was always pleasant, enthusiastic, wide eyed, thoughtful, eager to help and extremely competent. We got along well. But as the months passed, Ronnie gradually seemed to change. He wasn't always the cheerful person he had been, but who is? I noticed one day that he was wearing facial make-up, and while I thought it was "a little over the top," he probably was just experimenting. Later I realized he was hiding bruises.

A few months later, Ronnie told me he was going to quit his job. He and his partner were going to move to the West Coast. Time passed and then one day, to my surprise, in a telephone call from Human Resources I was told Ronnie had quit his job. He hadn't told me personally or said goodbye.

A few days later I received a call from a young woman, who said she was a friend of Ronnie. She said it was a secret but Ronnie was in a hospital on Chicago's north side. His partner had beaten him up and thrown him down a set of stairs. Ronnie's injuries included a broken leg, facial and body bruises, and other injuries, but he would recover. His partner had taken him to the ER and told them Ronnie had been in a car accident. She gave me Ronnie's room number.

I left work early that day and went to see Ronnie where he was registered as a patient using his partner's name. That worried me!

Ronnie lay in the hospital bed, his face discolored, swollen and bruised, one of his legs in traction, one eye half closed. Thankfully, his partner was not present. I was stunned. Ronnie looked at me; he seemed to be in pain. "Thank you for coming," he said.

"What happened?" I asked. Ronnie didn't answer. "I'm going to be okay," he said.

He didn't sound at all okay. There was a heavy waterfall of tears and pain hidden behind his words.

"You know you have to stop this!" I said. Ronnie turned away from me towards the wall.

"Do you realize what has happened, Ronnie? You are here, in the hospital, under an assumed name."

"I don't have health insurance," he said. Good grief! He had been working for me in a hospital and had no insurance.

"This is illegal. This is insurance fraud. It is not only that you have allowed yourself to be beaten up and hurt. Ronnie, you have given up your name. You have given away who you are! Whatever else you do, Ronnie, do not give away the person you are. Don't give away yourself."

He didn't answer.

"You are a good person, Ronnie! Never give up on yourself or who you are! You must change what is happening to you! You must!"

Before he could respond, his doctor entered the room. He greeted Ronnie warmly, calling him by his partner's name.

"Goodbye, " I said to Ronnie. "Remember what I said. You can call me."

Outside his room I waited until the doctor left and stopped him. "I need to talk to you," I said.

The doctor hesitated.

"He's not the person he is pretending to be," I said. "He needs help. He is being abused."

The doctor looked at me and put up one hand, his palm up toward me. "Don't say anything more. I don't want to know anything about this. If he's someone other than who he says he is, I do not want to know about it. I'll help him as much as I can, but I do not want to know about it."

I nodded and left.

If I did more, Ronnie would be in trouble with the hospital and insurance company. I did not want to make things worse and I did not want to tangle with his partner, who, I feared, was dangerous. If only Ronnie was a woman, I thought. There were safety nets, battered women programs and fine organizations that helped abused women. I had no idea how to help a young man in this situation.

Ronnie never called me. I want to believe that if not right away, Ronnie would somehow find the strength within himself, and do what was necessary to be the person he was meant to be. Would he stay in Chicago, move to the west coast, perhaps go back to Indiana? I did not know.

Ronnie was no longer my employee, and he was in the care of another hospital. I wished him well. Once he had confided in me that he believed in angels. I prayed that with their help Ronnie would find the necessary strength and courage.

From the Rear View Mirror:

About 25 years have passed since I visited Ronnie. Looking back, I think there has been great progress in reducing prejudice and increasing acceptance of non-heterosexual people.

We need to protect men as well as women who have been abused or need protection, whatever their situation. I understand that existing programs for abused women now also serve abused men.

It was up to Ronnie to make needed changes! When I last saw him, he was still capable of moving forward, away from being a victim, but obviously it would be very difficult, if not impossible unless he learned to love and care for himself!

I hope Ronnie is alive, that he is okay! I hope Ronnie now has a kind and loving husband and a job he enjoys!

THE DECLARATION OF *INTER*DEPENDENCE

Tale 14: My Place and Yours

Before retiring from Swedish Covenant Hospital in Chicago I interviewed the chief physician of the hospital. By now we had worked together for several years and we got along well. "Doc" was a renaissance kind of person who had a collection of antique medical instruments. The interview went well, as expected. After interviewing him, together we looked at the old medical instruments in his locked glass cabinet; he explained their purposes and how they were used.

"They look...like instruments of torture," I said. He nodded and replied, "As will our instruments of healing look to people in the future," a fascinating but somewhat frightening assessment. I hoped to find a way to quote his remark in the article, but I couldn't think of a way. When the interview was over, I thanked him for his time and was about to leave when he said, "Joy, do you know what I like about you?"

"No," I said, turning toward him, anticipating a compliment. Perhaps he was glad the interview had not taken too long.

"You know your place," he said, smiling.

I nodded. (Whenever a remark can be interpreted as either a compliment or an insult, choose the compliment!) I felt acknowledged. Perhaps the good doctor realized that I had no desire to be in a higher social position or higher in the hospital's power structure. If that was what he meant, he was correct. My place is where I am. Where else would I want to be?

"Thank you," I said.

From the Rear View Mirror

Social status is measured in dollars and written in labels or sometimes in abbreviated addresses. We are each more or less, better or worse, higher or lower than other individuals. However as human beings, we are equals.

All of us on our earth journeys are having experiences we chose. Each of us is a student of whatever life has to teach us. I believe Doc understood and valued that.

I may know my place. I love my place. That day I also realized it was time for me to move on.

Interdependence produces independence.

Tale 15: Jack's Complaint

Jack Galter was first and foremost a drummer in several big bands. Later, he became a businessman and then a philanthropist. He and his wife Dollie were the wealthiest people I ever knew and some of the most down-to-earth!

I knew Jack for only the last few years of his life (he died in 1993). But I recall many gala events when he would take the flatware next to his plate and use the glassware on the table to add to the orchestra's beat. As a great benefactor of many causes, he could join drummers in whatever band happened to be playing for whatever philanthropic cause—such as The Heart Association, The Rehabilitation Institution, or Swedish Covenant Hospital where I first came to know Jack and Dollie.

When they were first married, the couple had only $100, But when I knew them, they lived in a penthouse on top of a building in the heart of Chicago's gold coast, with a private elevator to the top floor. According to the newspaper, their foundation gave more than $100 million to charities, primarily in the Chicago area. Jack had owned the Spartus clock company but the Galter wealth came primarily through his real estate transactions, initially buying properties that lost value due to the depression.

It may now have been about 90 years ago that Jack drove into the parking garage next to the Carriage House in Chicago and was turned away.

"Sorry," The man in the booth said, "We don't allow people like you to park here." (Jews were not allowed!)

Jack found another place to park that day, but when he got into his office, he called the owner of the parking garage, someone he happened to know, and told him what had happened.

"Why don't you buy it, Jack?" the owner said. "Then it will never happen again."

So, Jack did.

From the Rear View Mirror:

I love the justice of this story! Injustice doesn't always go that well. But sometimes it does and for that I celebrate!

But do not misunderstand. Jack did not buy the parking garage to show his wealth, or his power, or to "win" or "get even." It was not retaliation. Jack realized the parking garage was an excellent investment and should serve people without regard to their religion. After having such an unpleasant prejudicial experience, Jack was presented with an excellent opportunity. For many, many years the parking garage has provided parking convenience to countless others and still does.

Tale 16: Goodbye Dollie!

In January 1990 I suddenly had time on my hands. After arriving at my new job at Swedish Covenant Hospital, the decision was made not to proceed with the fundraising project for which I had been hired. The decision was made to wait until priorities were reviewed. It turned out to be an excellent decision!

The new Life Center was just being completed. It was the first major fitness center in Chicago that was sponsored by a hospital. Cardiac rehabilitation was a major emphasis of the new center. One of our doctors had helped Jack Galter, now in his 80s, exercise on a stationary bicycle and after exercising, Jack felt better.

A few days after meeting the Galters at a luncheon in the President's office I telephoned and arranged to visit Jack and Dollie in their foundation offices on a lower floor where they lived in a skyscraper gold coast penthouse. Dollie was then in her 80s, in a wheelchair, but otherwise healthy. I liked her immediately. She had so much energy and vitality!

Because the campaign had been put off, I had some extra time. I began to invite Dollie out. Soon we were going out about once a week for lunch and then stopping at places she liked to visit. Dollie did not care much for fancy shops, expensive restaurants or other gold coast stores in the neighborhood. She enjoyed good soup and resale shops.

Dollie liked to eat in good delicatessens and ethnic restaurants in her favorite Chicago neighborhoods. Excellent design and quality were most likely to be found in resale or small shops.

For the next ten years, I would pick up Dollie and her caregiver, toss the wheelchair in the back of my hatchback and we would be off. Typically, after lunch we would go shopping at a resale or specialty shop. Dollie liked to help me make selections and was very good at selecting a particular dress or an unusual or inexpensive item. She seldom purchased anything for herself, even if it were inexpensive.

The Galters made a naming gift to the new fitness center. We had an Open House to introduce the Galter Life Center to the community. Nearly a thousand people of all ages and from various ethnic groups came to see the center. Especially surprising was how many and how much older people were interested in healthy living. (A marketing study had indicated something like our best prospect was a 35-year-old Caucasian woman with one child.) While there must have been a few of them who joined, there were many more 72-year-old gentlemen and women. The facility was inviting with an upstairs running track surrounded by windows overlooking the grounds, and attractive swimming and therapeutic pools downstairs.

I never asked Dollie for a gift or a donation. I kept her informed of what was happening at the hospital and Life Center and what was needed. I left it to her and her attorneys to decide when they wanted to make a gift and for what purpose. Over almost a decade the Galters gave approximately eight million dollars to the hospital. The Galter Medical Center and the Galter Life Center were both named for them. The effect on the hospital's growth and the extended, improved service to the community was immeasurable.

Dollie learned quite a bit about fundraising and regularly volunteered. She helped set up a marathon to benefit breast cancer research. Dollie was amazed at the detail that such an event required of staff. "I always thought it just meant putting on your shorts and showing up! There's a lot more to it!" she said. Once when asked what she liked about the hospital, Dollie said "You feel like they not only like you but that they know you."

Dollie and I always had fun. She became involved with virtually all the receptions and activities at the hospital. My husband Don and I were often invited to several other gala events in Chicago supported by the Galter Foundation. We also welcomed Dollie to our home. Special dinners and events honoring the Galters were often held at the Drake Hotel. As a young woman Dollie had worked at the front desk of the Drake Hotel, sending and receiving telegrams.

Swedish Covenant Hospital was part of the Covenant Church, and it was a surprise to many that a Jewish foundation would give money to a Christian organization. Jack and Dollie were generous supporters of Jewish causes, but their interest and friendships were wide. One of the delights of the hospital and Galter Life Center was that it served a multiplicity of ethnic identities on the north side of Chicago. The diverse Swedish Covenant Hospital staff spoke more than 40 languages, and at least 3 full time interpreters were available to Emergency Room patients. At the Galter Life Center, all signage was in Korean as well as English.

As a child Dollie had lived in San Francisco. Fortunately, her family moved away the day before the major earthquake. She recalled how a maid dressed her and another little girl in white and had them sit in the parlor to wait for Hayley's comet to come and take their lives.

I was careful to see that money never had anything to do with our relationship. It had to do with enjoying each other's company and loving life. Dollie knew her power and was not afraid to use it; her power was not based on ego. She was knowledgeable, intelligent, fair, well-spoken and highly intuitive.

Dollie was an egalitarian, and had a lot of good common sense as well as a sharp sense for business. Occasionally, when we did go to a fine restaurant, she would check things out by talking to the hat check girl, the waiter, or a doorman. "How have things been going?" she would ask. "It doesn't seem you are as busy as usual. Do you know why?"

There were attempts to take advantage of Dollie. She was too smart to fall for something obvious, but she was not immune from people trying, and in rare situations she experienced betrayal.

Dollie's family situation was difficult. She did not get along with her only daughter, nor communicate with two of her four grandsons and their families. Only one grandson seemed close to her. He became both a friend and Galter Life Center board member. Too much or too little money often affects family relationships in negative ways.

I had made the decision to retire early, and move to the Upper Peninsula at the turn of the century. As the scheduled time became closer and closer, I realized how difficult it was going to be to leave Dollie. Yes, she had many other friends, but we had a special relationship. There is something so incredibly beautiful about a friendship beyond barriers, where we are one in spite of differences. But I also knew in my heart that I needed to stay on my own path.

The last time I saw Dollie she was in the hospital. At age 97, she was dying, and had several tubes going in and out of her. I was afraid she might not be allowed to die. I felt it was right for me to leave, and so I said goodbye.

Philanthropy literally means loving people. It is always best when it lives up to its name. Many gifts are made for other reasons: obligation, ego, status symbol. Such were not the primary motivations of Jack and Dollie. Their gifts were made because of the need for them, because they loved people and they loved life. In spite of all the barriers we create, we share our humanity. We are all connected. We are one.

Many people on both ends of the financial spectrum value people based on how much wealth they have. Dollie knew who she was, and she understood and liked almost everyone! She loved people. Ordinary people.

I came back to Chicago to attend Dollie's funeral. Representatives from many of the organizations who literally received millions of dollars were present. Family members did not sit together. I did not see her daughter. There was no music. There was no humor. I did not feel Dollie's presence. She had left us. I loved her and I missed her.

Dollie had told me that she was not afraid to die. She was an excellent horseback rider; I believe she was in her 80s when she was thrown by a horse. Dollie suffered a head injury when she landed. But in that landing, she had a spiritual experience of being welcomed to another kind of existence. Dollie was aware of something even better, grander on the other side of this lifetime. It was such a beautiful experience that in a way she looked forward to it.

From the Rear View Mirror:

I am so blessed to have known Dollie and I will always be deeply grateful for her friendship. This tale is a tribute to her. It is odd that financial status is often what negates or qualifies relationships. Dollie never allowed that to happen. How weird, that money, while seldom discussed, was the basic reason for our having a relationship. It gives me hope. Some situations provide unintended opportunities to learn about life and essential equality.

Looking back, I realize how interdependent Dollie and I were. It was not contractual. We just liked each other and were both better off because of what we shared. It's that simple!

.

PART II:

Grundtvig's Principles, Folk Schools and Civil Rights

Walter Capps Predictions: the 21st Century

In 1992 my life was changed by a series of lectures at Danebod Folk Meetings in Tyler MN, given by Walter Capps (1934-1997), a professor and theologian from the University of California who became a U.S. Congressman. His topic was "The Future of Grundtvigianism," a surprising title to me because I grew up in a Grundtvigian household in Danish-American communities, and thought I knew a lot about N.F.S. Grundtvig (grunt-vee). He was an amazing philosopher, poet, educator and theologian, but didn't he belong to the past? What did Grundtvig's (1781-1872) philosophy and theology have to do with the future? I gradually learned that Walter Capps and Grundtvig both had a great deal to say about what it means to be a human being and creating a better future for all. (See Appendix for a short biography and description of N.F.S. Grundtvig's influence.)

At a time when most people expected to hear about a future world of ever-increasing improvements, Capps' lectures predicted multiple disasters. According to Capps, the 21st century would bring violence and injustice; environmental catastrophes; more racism, injustice and ethnic prejudice; decline in basic education; increased poverty; rampant displacement; and more suffering. According to Capps, governments throughout the world whether capitalist, socialist, dictatorships or communist were all failing humanity. Something different or in addition was needed.

Capps was very concerned about the lack of unity in our country. A faculty member in a major university, Walter Capps taught a popular class on the Vietnam War; 1000 students came year after year. He was aware of the lack of unity among the University's diverse student body and throughout the entire country. Without common values to unite us, it would be extremely difficult to meet the critical needs that he predicted.

But Capps was not a man without hope. He was looking for answers, values that could be shared to create better lives for all people and were accessible to all. He needed and wanted principles which could improve people's lives; they would need to be independent of any particular religion.

He found what he was looking for in the Danish theologian, poet, and educator, philosopher, N.F.S. Grundtvig, a controversial Lutheran clergyman who was committed to freedom of religion. His mantra is "Human First." While Grundtvig is not well known in the United States he is very well known to most Danes, even better known than Soren Kierkegaard or Hans Christian Andersen. The lives of these three men overlapped in time.

Capps was first led to Grundtvig by a question from one of his students who asked him, "Isn't anyone happy?" Capps took the students' question seriously, and in a visit to nearby Solvang, CA found what he considered an answer when he met several "Grundtvigian" Danes.

Capps, a non-Dane, was aware that Denmark is consistently at the top of worldwide polls when it comes to happiness. Grundtvig is seen as a major influence for the Danes' high ranking in the happiness department. Danes are not entirely without problems but they have a strong economy, excellent health, are well educated and quite comfortable with their government.

Grundtvig is known as the founder of folk schools. Many years ago, there was a folk school in Solvang, CA, a community which still projects a Grundtvigian influence.

Walter Capps developed friendships in the community and carefully began studying Grundtvig.

In Grundtvig's mantra, "Human First, then Christian" (or other religions), and in Grundtvig's massive works, Capps discovered what he identified as Grundtvig's four basic principles. They were independent of religion, had current relevance, and could bring well-being and happiness to people who followed them.

What does "Human First" mean?

It means we start with what we have in common: being human!

"Human First" is a factual statement of history. Humans were on earth long before there was religion.

People comes first, and then religion. It follows that life is first and foremost about being human! It is important for human beings to be aware of the fullness of earthly life, and to acknowledge the humanity of others.

Enjoy life, enjoy nature, live deeply and enjoy the world!

We are fortunate that Capps was able to distill Grundtvig's huge number of mind-blowing writings into only four principles that were critically needed in today's world and met Capps requirement in being acceptable to people of all backgrounds and religions.

Perhaps inspired by Grundtvig who was twice elected to the Danish legislature, Capps entered politics. He ran successfully for the House of Representatives. Elected to congress as a Democrat in 1994 Walter Capps at age 62, was the oldest freshman congressman, and the first Democrat to be elected in his California district since World War II. At the Danebod folk school meeting in 1992, he remarked that he wished he could run as a Grundtvigian.

Tragically, Walter Capps never saw the new millennium. He died unexpectedly on October 28, 1997, from a heart attack at Dulles airport after only three years in office. His wife Lois Capps, a nurse by profession with no political experience, stepped in and was elected six terms to the U.S Congress before retiring.

While Capps was correct about difficulties in this new

millennium, I believe we are now entering a new paradigm. There are signs of turnings in new directions, recognizing and honoring our interdependence, efforts to counteract, ameliorate or prevent further destruction due to climate change, and more appreciation for life itself. While subject to free will, a new realignment with commitment to truth and grace seems to be occurring.

Grundtvig's Four Principles

Capps four principles are: (1) Affirmation of Life, (2) Stay as Close as Possible to Nature (3) The Goodness and Beauty of Ordinary Life and (4) Lifelong Learning.

1.   Affirmation of Life

Affirm life! Life is an adventure! Life is fantastic! It is especially interesting in our time, when immense changes are occurring. You and I are meant to be here!

Find joy in creation, honor life's goodness.

Recognize and celebrate the goodness of creation. Accept and love the world as it is, realizing the world needs to be transformed. Do not concentrate on what is wrong with the world. You and I are here to help transform it! Do not get lost in a constant fabrication of what should/could be. Enjoy the world as it is.

Human beings are not mechanistic wooden puppets. We are real live human beings who have free will! Free will! Do you have any idea what that means? We get to do or have what we want! We can make what we believe needs to happen to actually happen!

But we are accountable! Let's go for it!

Enjoying life is not about perfection, but rather about living in gratitude, having hope, taking pleasure in what you have, cherishing who you are rather than self-judging yourself about what you lack.

Live in gratitude. Be thankful you are alive—from the top of your head down to the end of your live toes!

Consider all that you are, all that you have and give thanks.

Give thanks! Give more thanks! Give even more thanks!! Gratitude is a precious state of mind! It is the most important ingredient for having a tasty, happy life.

Meet the challenges that come to you with gratitude. These are opportunities to learn! If nothing else, the possibility for growth makes a situation more welcome.

Even when your life is not going well, even when life is painful, there is much to live for! This is wonderful world! Take the long view. Wisdom takes a while to develop. Give it a chance!

Look to children and adolescents for new energy. They are new beings! Fresh troops from the universe! Learn from them!

Design/create your own environment. Do not get stuck in someone else's view of life. Responding to heavy emotions with even heavier emotions adds energy to problems. Don't add energy to it. You have the power to choose your own emotions. You can select compassion over anger, choose understanding over criticism.

Embrace reality! This is a world where nearly everyone experiences a broken heart. This is a world where children are hungry, people are tortured. It is a world where there is deception, lying, cheating, illnesses, and pain. A world of temptations to be something other than who and what we are. It is a world we can transform, by honoring who we are and following our life purposes.

This world is one of incredible beauty, kindness and caring— a world where there is helpfulness, sweetness, fellowship, and joy. It is a world where there is gentleness, healing, ecstasy, understanding, sharing, enjoyment, and bliss. A world of care, renewal, sanctity, integrity and truth.

We are on a special holiday, a mission. We are stopping in

Port Earth for a short while. Cosmically speaking, we are here only for a stopover, a fortnight, or a blink! Let's enjoy it while we are here, do and be what we came to do and be!

Be aware that there are others in the world—every other life is equally important to yours. But your chief responsibility is to care for and be yourself. Know and value who you are; what you are. Be the person only you are. See yourself as light.

Learn to live each day in enjoyment; learn to live in community. Be part of earthly transformation and healing. Give thanks for your wonderful LIFE!

2. Stay as Close as Possible to Nature

We are part of nature. We are made of the same "stuff."

Evidently, the elements that make up our human bodies were formed as a result of a supernova (star explosion) about six billion years ago, forming our sun, earth and other planets in the universe.

The elements created by star explosions are found in nature, and these same elements are also within our bodies. We are like the stars. You and I are made of star-material.

We are cut from the same cloth, part of the same cosmos!

You, I, him, her—all of us are part of one magnificent creation.

We're not on just any old planet! This is our place!

Our earth home is a relative of other planets. Let's take care of our home! She is incredibly beautiful. Enjoy the earth; enjoy being here.

Run. Dance. Walk. Jump. Swim. Sail. Lie down on the grass. Look up at the sky at white foamy clouds softening the sun's rays. It has taken us a long time to get here. Enjoy the earth's sights, smells and tastes!

Consider the dandelions. Consider the trees. What kind of world would we have without trees? Without dandelions? Consider the streams and brooks, the rivers, lakes and oceans. The rocks! Consider the dolphins and whales, the chickadees and doves, the crows and sparrows! Consider sunrises, sunsets, mountains and valleys, deserts and rainforests. All are gifts! It is up to us to receive them, to experience the joy of our incredible gifts.

Take a walk. Send a loving blessing to a tree that you meet along the way. Wait a second or two. Large or small, young or old, oak or evergreen, the tree will return its unique blessing to you. Each tree, each blessing is different from any other tree's blessing. Receive it throughout your entire body! Be thankful!

Thank you, beautiful tree!!

Trees protect us, shelter us, nourish us in their very breathing. They purify our wastes. Trees communicate with one another in ways we do not understand. They are alive! What would we do without them?

You are in the wind, the waves, the rocks, the pebbles and the sand. The birds, the trees, the insects and bears. Bushes, weeds, flowers and peas are your siblings. Along with us, the grass, the clouds, the sky, the sea and earth, are all part of creation. Even if you are visiting from another galaxy, while you are here, you are made of earthly elements.

We would not be on earth if we were not part of it.

Nature cannot be anything apart from us, nor can we be apart from nature. We know both pain and joy as earthlings. We are dependent on our Mother Gaia, whom we love dearly. We will no longer neglect her.

Nature provides our food, our drink. Nature sustains and

upholds us. Sometimes she causes harm, even destroys what we have made, but Mother Gaia cannot and will not destroy our souls. She cannot destroy our spiritual selves; she creates far more than she destroys.

It is our time.

Everything in nature is part of the whole—you, me, we are each a piece of this earth puzzle. Everything, everyone contributes to the whole!

Wherever you live, tenement or tower, mansion or hut, look out the window each morning and experience the incredible beauty, the power of the natural world, no matter how grand or how small the vision. Know you are part of it. Be part of it. Do not be apart from it.

Respect and love the earth! Mother Gaia is aging!

She has worked hard for us for eons and eons! She has not been treated well. It is our time. We must care for her and not allow others to abuse her. Without her, we have no life on earth!

Mother Gaia has a temperature. She is dehydrated and worn out! She has a bad infection and her respiratory problems are so severe she sometimes needs more oxygen!

If we don't do something to help her, the infection may worsen!

What on earth happened to her? Mother Gaia is suffering from scarring, "skin" eruptions, problems with elimination, wounds that don't heal. What has caused such distress? Consuming self-interests have increased to a point where it is toxic —earth is a closed system.

Industrialization has contributed to human advancement, but in the process, it caused harm— spoiling our seas, raping the land, crushing Mother Gaia's ability to recover on her own. Now she has been given too many antibiotics which are causing problems with her elimination system. How do we heal her?

Mother Gaia is not being passive about her health. After all, she is a mom. Mother Gaia is fighting back and will continue to do so, but she needs help. We must take better care of her. True, every life is terminal, including Mother Gaia, but she has several good eons left to live—generations of human beings are waiting to follow us! It is not too late to save her and provide her with a better quality of life. We need to help her regain as much health as possible so that she may live many more light years.

It is not too late to let her know how much we love her. We are all interdependent with each other and interdependent with the earth.

We are all healthier when we are all healthier. We are all richer when we are all richer! We are all better off when we are all better off.

Nature's most important lesson is humility. The forces of nature teach us that we didn't create Mother Gaia. We have accomplished marvelous ways, but they are just ways of doing. We take pride, and are even giddy over our many wondrous inventions— telephones, rocket ships, x-rays, computers, indoor plumbing, test tube babies, miracle medications, tooth implants. We made them all and they are good!

We take pride in making ways of doing things and occasionally even improve on nature. But we did not create nature! We did not lay the cornerstone when the morning stars sang together! (Job 38). We did not create the elements from which our bodies are made, and which we share with all of nature as well as the stars. Yes, with help from each other, we can put things together in creative ways from what is provided. We are glad to do that!

The only way to end further destruction is for us to become

a more earth-caring, people-caring, animal and vegetation-caring species that pays loving attention to the welfare of the earth and everything on it—human beings, plants, animals, minerals.

What we do to others we do to ourselves.

3. The Goodness and Beauty of Ordinary Life

Every life is both ordinary and extraordinary. Notice the goodness of ordinary people! Someone smiled at you, or held a door open for you, or called you, or helped or offered help, perhaps advised you, or just delighted you by the way they were. Before you go to sleep, think of that individual, and give thanks.

Each of us is *"one* in a million" and each of us is "one in a *million."* And these two truths occur at the same time!

Isn't that fantastic? It's like occupying two places at the same time. You can be both—humble and special at exactly the same instant! Go for it!

Believe in ordinary people. Ordinary people are fantastic; they are the stability of our world. Do not pity people. Do not feel sorry for them. See them as resources. See them as divine human beings, potential resources for helping others. If you can help them—help them, but do not pity them. They are extraordinary.

My friend Kwi Esei said, we once loved people and used things. But we have come to love things and use people. A modest amount of seeing ourselves as machine-like is helpful. After all, humans created machines as ways to better accomplish things. We share functional similarities, but we are not machines. We have souls. Souls are much more than intelligence.

Unfortunately, we had a misguided response to the Industrial Age. We were so impressed with the machinery that many people became as machine-like as possible. We over defined our bodies, our actions, our society in mechanistic terms.

We went too far. The results are excessive materialism; disproportionate individualism without regard for others; perception of nature only as something for use; treating people as objects (machines) rather than equal human beings, limiting our understanding and knowledge about who we are.

We can manifest equality by honoring one another instead of using each other. We must each enlarge our own little world, honor our own ways, but welcome others and accept their ways. We are all interdependent. Open your world to someone new, someone different from you, with whom you seek compatibility.

Love is beyond approval; love is far beyond agreement. If we don't love people as they are, hoping they will somehow change, we don't really love them. The same is true for our world. Be kind to people who are immature or untested. They have much to learn.

Hate is dissolved by acts of love. Envy is annulled by identifying and achieving one's own goals. Unkindness or rudeness is neutralized by acts of kindness and thoughtfulness.

Each of us has an ego to deal with. Grundtvig referred to ego as the human knot. If we wish to grow, our knots must be untied. But untying one's knot is a tricky process and one which we need to do ourselves. Each of us must do our own untying. Do not untie another person's knot unless clearly invited to do so. It is not your business!

Ego applies to everyone, ordinary or extraordinary!

It also applies to groups such as families, companies, countries as well as individuals. All such groups have egos. Children, babies through teenagers, come with fresh, new information from their pre-birth worlds. Listen to them; learn from them. Do your best to nurture them, realizing how important the first seven years are to a child's development. Know you will fail them in some way, no matter what you do. Children misinterpret; we all have our limitations.

Work with your hands. There is great integrity in working with one's hands. Engage in the arts, crafts, music, woodwork, cooking, writing, cleaning, wood carving, other projects. Make something special with your hands—color, polish, paint, erase, push, pick up, mark, wave, point, pull, shape, move, lift, tie, untie, match, design, catch, funnel, take, give—it is all done with hands. Love your hands!

One of the reasons Denmark has fewer problems than many other countries is there exists almost no poverty. One of Grundtvig's most famous sayings comes from a poem or song. "In this lies our wealth, on this tenet we draw that few are too rich, and still fewer too poor." (N.F.S. Grundtvig, "Far Higher are mountains elsewhere on earth"[3])

While the United States does not have an economic system to eliminate poverty, changes are being considered to address income equality. The imbalance of income in the United States has become unhealthy! Sadly, 41.4% of Americans are classified as low-income or low-income families. The top 1% earners make 20 times more than the bottom 90%. The 1% have drained $50 trillion from the bottom 90% over the last 45 years. And it is becoming worse. (2021 income Inequality statistics, *Spend Me Not*).

This imbalance is not a tenable situation. Hopefully, new tax legislation will make some improvements, but many more major changes are necessary.

Happiness? Find meaning and happiness in relationships with one another and in doing what you are called to do.

---

[3] *Poem 91, page 190 Living Wellsprings The Hymns, Songs and Poems of N.F.S.Grundtvig, Edward Broadbridge (translator and editor), Aarhus University Press, 2015*

4. The Principle of Lifelong Learning and Education

Education for life is necessary in order for democracy to survive and thrive.

While Grundtvig had a great respect and a close relationship with the Danish monarchy, he realized that Democracy was the movement of the future. Democracy is dependent on education. To Grundtvig that meant an education not only to make a living, but an education to live and enjoy life! Grundtvig is founder of the Folk Schools and is credited with establishing the concept of Lifelong Learning.

Grundtvig saw how much a common education about life was needed for all people if Democracy was to be successful in Denmark. He was alarmed by the brutality of the French revolution and he did not want Denmark to have that kind of experience. Grundtvig did not view the peasant class as inferior but rather as people rich with wisdom, talent, abilities, and common sense who needed to be properly educated. The peasants represented great potential for the country.

What if we approached poverty and those whom we consider needy as people who have much to teach us and contribute? We are a nation which has benefited by having immigrants from many ethnicities and countries.

Grundtvig was interested in more than book learning. The purpose of education is not to mold the masses, but rather to challenge and empower ordinary people, assisting them to grasp their identity, understand their purposes in life, look after their own affairs as they pursue their interests and work together. Living education, the spoken word, and discussion classes were most important in the school for life which included a "living interaction" between students and teachers. This was necessary for ordinary people if they were to have political and cultural power in a democratic society.

School days began and ended with singing and the days included storytelling, reading, writing, math, history, current events, crafts, and lectures. Small groups learned to work together on projects and all students helped out with everyday chores of group living.

Lifelong Learning: Lands of the Living

Grundtvig has sown more seeds throughout the world than we can know! It is fascinating to see how his ideas are practiced in different cultures. Grundtvig lived at a time when nationalism was just beginning to blossom.

Denmark lost world influence in losing the war to Prussia, but the Danish people gained power in individual and community growth. "What is outwardly lost must be inwardly gained".[4]

With the folk school movement, the Danish people became proud of their lives, their history, their culture, and the earth. They came to love who they were, understand their history and prepare for the future.

Rather than nationalism, we now live in a time when we are affected by globalization. Nations and their governments are losing some of their hold on its citizens. This is our time to become more global while remaining local and national as we celebrate our unique histories, learn more about other cultures, and work to resolve international concerns about peace, health and climate issues.

The United States has a unique role in this effort, since our country is composed of many different races and creeds. Proud of our individual heritages, we realize the need to respect all heritages and cultures, develop the international community, exchange ideas, and blossom as a new world.

In the 19th Century Denmark needed a "living education" to establish Democracy in modern Denmark. We need similar educational methods to establish a global world. Fruitful seeds of

---

[4] *"What is outwardly lost must be inwardly gained." quote attributed to Grundtvig from poet Peter Holst, 1872.*

education for life and living have been sown around the world!

There are no better examples of the importance and educational worth of Grundtvig's four principles than in in various folk schools around the world where they have significant impact in empowering the students, developing their talents, teaching them about their countries' history, current events, how to enjoy life, be part of a community and contribute to society. While there are different races and ethnicities, age groups, backgrounds and needs, the folk schools share the four principles.

In 2018 I attended a symposium on the international influence of N.F.S. Grundtvig---Voices from "Lands of the living." It was held at the University of London where 50 community leaders, educators, priests, scholars and students from 14 countries gathered--Bangladesh, China, Denmark, England, Finland, Hungary, India, Japan, Nigeria, Norway, the Philippines, South Korea, Sweden and the USA. A representative from each of these countries talked about Grundtvig and their folk school experiences.

There are both similarities and differences in the various schools. Surprising to me was how many of the schools show the importance of the mother tongue to the folk school's educational process. How interesting! The same folk schools stress the preparation of participation in a future multicultural global society! Perhaps the mother tongue is an important tool in formulating the legacies of the various cultures and actually helps create a rich multicultural world!

Organized by Mark Bradshaw Busbee from Sanford University in Birmingham, AL and Anders Holm from Copenhagen's University's Faculty of Theology, the symposium showed how Grundtvig's teachings have informed educational movements around the world.[5]

The following pages are about folk schools described in lectures on "Lands of the Living" showing Grundtvig's influence throughout the world.

The various folk schools show the extent to which N.F.S. Grundtvig's values and principles are known, taught and practiced in various ways throughout the world. They are manifestations of equality.

1. India—presented by Reghu Rama Das. Mitraniketan, a folk high school, "People's College" in India, is designed to educate and empower students and community members, and promote rural development. Mitraniketan's principles and practices draw from the ideas of Gandhi and Tagore as well as Arthur Morgan of the USA and N.F.S. Grundtvig. Its educational mission is to promote the progress of society through the development of the entire individual. Students reflect upon life experiences, develop interest in grassroots democracy, and acquire skills leading to employment, personal and leadership training. The school responds to a major need where village women design their own programs, engage in micro (savings and loan) credit, work together in self-help groups, and develop their skills through leadership and activities which improve their livelihood.

---

[5] *Voices from "Lands of the Living": Summaries and Conclusions from the 2018 Symposium on the International Influence of N.F.S. Grundtvig, Thorstein Balle, of the University of Copenhagen summarized the conference presentations, listing five categories of folk schools outside of Denmark according to their purpose: 1. those that stress a national dimension, an understanding of history or ideas about democracy; 2. an emancipatory dimension from social or political oppression; 3. the individual dimension such as , personal development; and 4. the knowledge and skill dimension.*

2. Bangladesh – presented by Tanvir Mokammel, Director of the Bangladesh Film Institute, who started a cultural school for the poorest, lowest class rural children in southern Bangladesh in the Khulna district. Tanvir's cultural school for poor children teaches song, dance, play-acting, painting, and using computers which the normal schools do not teach. History is pivotal to the learning process. Tanvir states, "From Grundtvig's ideas of *Folkelighed*, freedom and civil liberty, we the people living in lesser democracies like Bangladesh where we struggle to build up democratic institutions and democratic values, can learn a lot."

3. Janos Szigeti Toth spoke on "The case of Hungary: The impact of Grundtvig' educational ideas." Beginning in 1990, in Hungary, the concept of "folk high school" swept Hungary. "Folk High schools helped re-establish education for the people and revival measures that resist subversion of education into mass propaganda for political indoctrination. Folk High Schools have never been more important than today in Hungary, as we are witnessing a post-2010 authoritarian turn."

4. Melanie Lenehan, Principal and CEO of Fircroft College, Birmingham, England where 109-year-old historic buildings and grounds generate a sense of safety, security, retreat and refuge for people who are fleeing from traumatic life experiences — domestic violence, homelessness, alienation or unemployment. Connections with others are mutual, creative, energy-releasing and empowering for all participants. Teachers and learners are perceived as equals. In 2018 Fircroft was rated the top in student satisfaction out of England's 190 colleges.

5. "Finding NFS Grundtvig in the U.S." was presented by Vicky Eiben, founding board member of Driftless Folk School in Viroqua WI, USA. The school builds on the rural, agricultural heritage of the area, the immigrants, indigenous people and the geological and natural history of the region. Classes include blacksmithing, stargazing, folk dancing, herb gathering and homesteading skills.

6. Kachi A Ozumba spoke on "Grundtvig's Educational Ideas in Nigeria." The folk school movement in Nigeria was founded by the speaker's father, Dr. Kachi Ezogbuna Ozumba, in the early 1980's. Students are educated not just to make a living but also to live a useful and satisfactory life, develop a sense of self-worth, cultural pride, active citizenship, cooperative spirit, initiative, resourcefulness, critical thinking, fairness, tolerance and community spirit. The Grundtvig Institute in Nigeria, founded in 1984 has 500 students. It has a residential post-secondary school offering the Awareness Curriculum alongside vocational training in Catering, Home Management, Fashion, Textile Design, Computer Studies, Office Technology and Management. The International Secondary School founded in 1998 has 600 students, offers its Awareness Curriculum alongside national and international academic secondary school curricula. Both schools have been oversubscribed since 2016.

7. Edicio G. dela Torre presented "Philippine Encounter with Grundtvig." Edicio Torre, a Catholic priest, was arrested twice after martial law was imposed in 1972, and spent nine years in various military prisons until released when democracy was restored in 1986. Edicio advocates three programs to achieve popular democracy, community organizing, popular education and grassroots leadership. In 1992 he set up the Education for Life (ELF) Foundation to apply the ideas of Grundtvig and the Danish folk high

school to the Philippines with a core program for grassroots community leadership and empowerment. The program seeks to develop three core competencies of skills: 1. Communications 2. Negotiations and 3. Nonviolent conflict resolution.

8. Midori Sakaguchi on "Grundtvig's Influence on Japan:" Japan has had more than 100 year's history of Grundtvig influence, but did not have proper translations of Grundtvigs until recently. Mitsuru Shimizu published a translation of *School for Life* in 1996 and Christien Kold's book in 2007. He is best known as the director of the "Grundtvig Society in Japan." Naota Koike has written several books on Grundtvig.

9. Hae-jin Chung on "Grundtvig and the Education of South Korea:" A school influenced by Grundtvig is the Osan school founded in 1907. Osan school and Poolmoo Schools try to accept and practice Grundtvig's ideas of people's education, empowering people to enlighten themselves through education. "In 2016 Oh Yeon-ho founded an *efterskole* (Danish continuation school). His research on why Denmark is such a happy country, led him to the answer — it was because of Danish education and Grundtvig. Yang Seok-won, a people's high school, has at last been established in Korea. Its keywords are "self, freedom, community, empathy, life-itself and living by one's own reason."

10. Wen Gee presented a lecture titled "The Chinese Grundtvig: An Introduction to Lei Peihong's Pedagogical Contribution in China." Grundtvig was introduced to China in 1906. Before the People's Republic of China was founded in 1949, Grundtvig was popular with many Chinese educators, especially Lei Peihong, (1888- 1967) whose students called him the "Chinese Grundtvig." Lei

established Xijiang College, which had as its purpose to make education a reality for the people. He referred to the Danish folk high school to show the power of education to transform people for the sake of political, economic and cultural democracy. He wanted Xijiang College to provide living education that would take into account each student as a living person; he wanted teachers and students to have lively interactions and promote mutual learning while promoting formal education. He always wanted to expand informal education for the sake of the enlightenment of people and the improvement of their lives. Lei criticized educational processes that treat students mechanically. He promoted life-long education from the Chinese cultural perspective. Lei creatively contextualized Grundtvig's thoughts for his people. Only lifelong education can revive and lift up national spirits.

11. "Why Grundtvig still matters in Sweden" was presented by Tomas Rosengren: The Swedish folk high school turned 150 years old in 2018. The folk high schools in Sweden have a reputation for successfully helping students who failed the traditional education system, succeed in the folk high school. Folk High Schools in Sweden are in the business of making students become someone instead of something, and aware of their citizenship, not just in the local community, but as world citizens in a multicultural society. This is a new time when nationalism has turned into internationalism. The Folk High school has an important role to play over the course of the next 150 years.

12. "Grundtvig in Norway" by Synnove Sakura Heggem. Grundtvig has a very close relationship with Norway. The folk high school movement in Norway began in 1864 and Folk High Schools are still a vital part of Norwegian culture with about 80 schools. Norway also has Grundtvigian Free

schools for children. Nordal Rolfsen spread Grundtvig's ideas to Norwegian primary schools, ending strictly religious traditions for school training. Core values associated with the mother-tongue, song, poetry, patriotism, history and "cheerful Christianity" were central. Synnove's research on Grundtvig and sacred sound indicate that the nation's singing tradition is key to Nordic spirituality. (There are 32 Grundtvig hymns in the official hymn book.)

No one can over-estimate the effect N.F.S Grundtvig has had around the world. Seeds of equality have been planted throughout the world for generations.

North America Statistics: At the conference, Dawn J. Murphy presented research findings on the recent growth of folk education in the United States "Democracy, Leadership, and Education: Finding Grundtvig in the Modern United States Folk School Movement." According to Dawn Murphy: "As of July 2018, the Folk Education Association of American Folk Schools and the Folk School Alliance, have identified 82 currently active organizations including two in Canada. This data suggests that from 1990 to 2018, there has been an almost seven-fold increase in the number of folk schools in the United States.

Each folk school has its own dynamic, its own special purpose, and some have specialized in the arts, but they all honor Grundtvigian principles.

A shorthand version of the four principles:

Cherish Life

Cherish Nature

Cherish People (especially ordinary people)

Cherish Lifelong Learning!

If we honor these four principles, we will live a life that is *inter*dependent with people and with nature. Those who honor these principles will practice equality, help take care of the earth and will keep learning. They will appreciate life. It is "Human First." And it will make a tremendous difference.

When I have spoken to groups about Grundtvig's four principles I find that no one needs much convincing. Several people have told me they wish they had been raised with these concepts, or heard them before. This isn't new! These are principles which have roots in many cultures. We have these principles in common regardless of background, ethnicity or religion, but we need to practice them.

Other Major Folk School Experiences

When I visited Denmark in 2013 and interviewed individual Grundtvigians, I also visited four folk schools--The Teachers' Training School in Ollerup, The Senior Folk High School at Rude Strand, The Gymnastic Folk High School at Ollerup, and an Effterskole. My purpose was to obtain a first hand understanding of how Danish Grundtvigians view Grundtvig in modern times.

I quickly learned what an important role Grundtvig has today! His views are highly respected, widely discussed, and constantly quoted in the newspaper.

My own experiences with the Grundtvigian way of life came from growing up in my home and in Danish American communities. I went to Grand View College which was founded by Danish Immigrants and still has a bit of a folk school ethos to it, but it is now a university. I then went on to Shimer College which had many Grundtvigian attributes such as discussion classes and considerable interchange between students and teachers.

The goal is not to make a living as much as it is to make a worthwhile lifetime of service and critical thinking. I learned later from Walter Capps that the University of Chicago educator who was responsible for the Shimer program, Robert Maynard Hutchins, had studied Grundtvig!

The Danebod Folk Meeting, where I met Walter Capps, meets annually each year in August and the subjects of lectures and small group sessions vary—but there is always room for singing, afternoon storytelling, language classes, lectures and discussions. Lecture topics are divergent at the folk meeting--the 2022 series for the included Artificial Intelligence, Russia's war in the Ukraine, Healthcare, the Dakota War and its Aftermath, Feminism, and Art as Self Discovery. The program is diverse, followed by a Q & A or comments.

Although Danebod Folk School in Tyler MN is no longer a residential program it continues to inspire many of us at the annual meeting, where the lifetime learning program continues to offer folk school type experiences. My husband and I will continue to attend folk school family camps at Danebod Folk School in Tyler MN and West Denmark in Luck, Wisconsin as often as we are able. The West Denmark and Danebod's intergenerational family camps include gymnastic or exercise programs, swimming, softball games, as well as folk dancing and skits.

Finally, an additional folk school program which we must celebrate! Many people in the United States do not know the profound effect that the Highlander Folk Schools had on the Civil Rights movement.

Highlander Research and Education Center (formerly the Highlander Folk School)

How ironic that it was in Denmark that I learned more about the connection between Grundtvigian folk schools and the Civil Rights movement than I learned in the United States.

In September, 1913 I arrived at Vartov, the center for my research project on what Danish Grundtvigians currently think about N.F.S. Grundtvig. Situated next to Copenhagen's city hall, Vartov is a large brick edifice built in 1724-1755. In Grundtvig's time it was a hospital for poor and elderly people. Grundtvig, who was controversial, was given a clergy position there, likely to place him away from public notice. But Grundtvig became very popular in his ministry at Vartov where he served from 1839 until his death in 1872. Many students came to hear him including Denmark's royalty along with many of his other followers.

When I arrived at Vartov, one of the first items I noticed was a large poster of Dr. Martin Luther King. While my Danish language is very limited, I could tell it was about Grundtvig's relationship to the Civil Rights movement. I was aware there was some connection, but knew little specifics.

To summarize the connection, consider Barack Obama's speech at a Nordic State Dinner given 3 years later:

President Obama's Speech about Grundtvig, May 13, 2016, Nordic Dinner Event

"Many of our Nordic friends are familiar with the great Danish pastor and philosopher Grundtvig who, among other causes, championed the idea of the Folk School — education that was not just made available to the elite, but to the many. Training that prepares a person for active citizenship improves society.

"Over time the Folk School Movement spread, including here to the United States. One of those schools was in the state of Tennessee. It was called the Highlander Folk School. At Highlander, especially during the 1950s, new generations of Americans came together to share their ideas and strategies for advancing civil rights, for advancing equality and justice. We know the names of some of those who were trained or participated in the Highlander school—Ralph Abernathy, John Lewis. Dr. Martin Luther King, Jr.

"They were all shaped in part by Highlander and the teachings of the great Nordic philosopher, and they ended up having a ripple effect on the Civil Rights Movement and ultimately on making America a better place. We would not have been here had it not been for that stone that was thrown in the lake and created ripples of hope that ultimately spread across the ocean to the United States of America. I might not be standing here were it not for the efforts of people like Ella Baker and the others who participated in the Highlander Folk School.

"So, that's just one small measure of the enormous, positive influence that our Nordic friends have had on our country. It's part of the reason why we so value your friendship, and I've said it before and I will repeat, they punch above their weight. In their values, in their contributions, not just to making their own countries function well, but to make the whole world a better place makes them one of our most valuable partners everywhere in the world. We are very grateful for the outstanding work that they do. So, I propose a toast: To the friendship between us and the values that we share, and that our nations keep standing together and mending in part for the moral universe and stretching for justice and peace and equality for all. Skál. Cheers."

Myles Horton
Highlander Folk School,
The Civil Rights Movement

Barack Obama may not have become president if it were not for the Highlander Folk School and there would not have been such a school without Myles Horton (1905-1990) the founder of the Highlander Folk School. In the early 60s I was a student at the University of Chicago Divinity School. While there, I attended St. Stephens', a church on the South side of Chicago, not far from campus, which had once been a Danish church with Grundtvig's roots.

The minister of the church 30 years prior was Enok Mortensen, a friend of my parents. A group of University of Chicago students, including Horton, made their way to the church basement of St. Stephen's initially to attend a folk dancing event, where they met Enok and Aage Moller, also a Lutheran minister. They learned that Horton wanted to create a school for Appalachian people, empowering them and helping them develop their abilities and skills to make a better life. They recommended he start a folk school for Applachian people!

Aage and Enok convinced Myles to go to Denmark, learn the language, and "get with the people." Horton was at first wary that a folk school could make such a difference in people's lives. "I was unable to reconcile the contributions of the democratization of Denmark attributed to the schools with the explanations of how it was done, so I decided to make an on-site investigation." Horton spent a year in Denmark where he visited folk schools. When he came back, Myles Horton founded the Highlander Folk School.

Initially, Horton was involved in unions. He organized help for striking coal mine workers in Tennessee, providing food and clothing. Horton was arrested but continued to write to newspapers.

When Horton was trying to form a coalition of farm workers, he realized that the racial barrier separated working people. Organizing the workers was impossible.

It was necessary to develop civil rights classes for both blacks and whites. The folk school decided to focus on school desegregation, voter education and voters' rights.

Horton was dedicated to teaching black and white students how they could challenge social, economic and political structures in a segregated situation.

Folk music played an important part of the school. At the Danish Folk School, Horton had learned the importance of group singing. Myles' wife, Zilphia Horton collected old songs including "We shall Overcome," an old Baptist hymn. A young Highlander student, Pete Seeger, and Zilphia altered the lyrics slightly and taught the song to the students. The verse "We are not Afraid" was added after the KKK persuaded the police to charge Horton and the school with subversive activities. Four teachers were arrested, found guilty and the school was closed based on the school's integrated classes which then was against Tennessee state law.

Horton was instrumental in launching "Citizenship Schools" across the South to teach African-Americans to read so they could pass the literacy test required for voting rights. It has been estimated that 100,000 students were able to vote due to citizenship schools which provided the basis for the organized civil rights movement in the South.

In 1955 Rosa Parks decided to sit where she pleased on a bus. This action sparked the Montgomery bus boycott, which helped strike down segregation in the South. Rosa had attended a two-week desegregation workshop at the Highlander High School a few months earlier that summer. Later she said that her time at

Highlander was the first time she lived in an atmosphere of equality with members of the white race. Her last visit to the Highlander School was in 1990 to attend the memorial for Myles Horton following his death.

Dr. Martin Luther King was the feature speaker of the Highlander Workshops in 1957, the 25th anniversary of Highland High School. In 1990 Highlander Folk School buildings mysteriously burned to the ground. In 1961 Horton opened the Highlander Research and Education Center and began fully transferring the leadership of the citizenship school to the Southern Christian Leadership Conference.

Unfortunately, racial problems did not end. On March 29, 2019 the center, which consists of about 10 buildings on a 200-acre campus in New Market, 20 miles east of Knoxville, was again the site of a mysterious blaze that destroyed the center's main office building. A white power symbol was found in the parking lot near the rubble of the main building. Today the Highlander Research and Education Center continues the work of Myles Horton.

Human First, Then Christian (or Other Religion)

While the "Human First" Grundtvigian principles are independent from religion, it does not follow that religion or spirituality are insignificant. Capps was looking for principles all people can subscribe to regardless of their religious backgrounds or affiliation. Of course, many people who subscribe to "Human First" are religious! We are of many different religions and we are glad people who do not subscribe to any religion can also support the four principles.

Religion can be divisive or extremely helpful.

Grundtvig advocated freedom of religion, but he was and is known as an intensely religious man who wrote sermons, hymns and poetry. He was not only a theologian but he also became a Bishop. He wrote or adapted 1500 hymns, which are still sung in many countries.

Freedom of religion was extremely important to Grundtvig. Today Denmark has a national church which is supported by the government, but taxpayers are not required to pay taxes if they choose not to belong to the Danish national church. Also, there is a process for establishing a new church of a different denomination if enough people in a locality wish to form one. Grundtvig's strong stand on freedom of religion is reflected in the Danish constitution which he helped develop.

Grundtvig respected other religions, and especially valued Judaism, the religion of Jesus. Grundtvig had little knowledge and experience with the Muslim religion and did not comment much on it. Grundtvig was an expert on Norse mythology, and is widely known in literary circles for his translation of Beowulf. Grundtvig's mother had shared Norse myths and stories with him and he also studied and wrote about Norse mythology.

Grundtvig admired the Vikings and was sensitive to what pagan religions meant to followers of pagan religions. He did not enthusiastically support mission work which destroyed cultural beliefs.

Today many people separate spiritual life from religious life. As for myself, I need both. I was raised in the Danish Lutheran Church based on Grundtvigian theology in the United States, the AELC, which merged into the larger Lutheran church in 1962, which merged again and eventually became the ELCA. Depending on where I was living, I also have been an Episcopalian. I have an Episcopalian certificate in Lay Ministry from the University of the South. I am currently a member of an ELCA Lutheran church in Albuquerque. I also accompany my husband to a local synagogue and take spiritual guidance from their services. Our five children practice different religions. Their spouses are diverse — Roman Catholic, Greek Orthodox, New Age, and reformed Judaism.

I value "organized religion" for its messages, ceremonies, music, continual support, friendships, leadership, wisdom, social actions, charitable activities and generally because it carries and guides us week after week, century after century.

I also value spiritual growth on a personal basis. Each day I meditate and also have a 20-minute spiritual practice which is necessary for me. Each morning I ask my soul, what is most important for me to do that day. Often, I ask for help and pray for people who are ill or need help. In the evening, when I go to bed, I visualize the best or most beautiful moment of the day and hold that moment and give special thanks. I thank God for such a wonderful day and pray for the concerns I have.

Developing your own spirituality and your own religious life is a fantastic and lifelong experience. I wish you all well on your spiritual journeys. Blessings!

Catastrophic Surprises in the First Quarter of the 21st Century

I wish Walter Capps (see page 80) had lived into the 21st Century. My guess is he would have been surprised. His predictions have come true! I am grateful for his warnings. His teaching the four Grundtvigian principles and lifting them up has been helpful in handling life's challenges. But the 21st century brought even more difficulties than what Capps predicted! We have endured unprecedented stress!

Since the relatively short time since the new millennium began in 2000, we have experienced three unexpected catastrophic major events and unprecedented, ruinous disasters from climate change.

The events:

(1) Covid 19 has killed over a million people in the United States and over 6 million people throughout the world.

(2) Russia invaded Ukraine and the entire globe is now affected by a bloody, cruel war.

(3) An insurrection of the United States Capitol on January 6, 2020 over unacceptance of the 2020 election results by the outgoing president, and his political party's unquestioning endorsement of the former president in virtually all matters, threatens democracy in the United States and around the world.

These incredible events have caused suffering, death, fear of the future as well as increased polarity in the United States. It is now extremely difficult if not impossible to unite the country. In addition, the entire globe is feeling the effects of climate change.

The overwhelming mamouth disasters caused by Hurricane Ian will take many years if not decades to resolve. Ian has created a new sense of our interdependence on nature and one another. The earthquakes in Turkey and Syria have cause irreperable damage and taken over 50,000 lives.

Climate change has caused a huge increase in forest fires, leaving thousands of people homeless. Much of the entire country is threatened by longer periods of drought; tropical storms create havoc; ice caps are melting and oceans are rising.

Everyone and everything is affected by climate change. We are interdependent which affects food supplies, transportation, health, jobs, animal and plant life, and the economy in general.

Some individuals, who in addition to the stress of Covid-19, war and politics, have suffered major personal losses due to climate change such as deaths of loved ones, destruction and loss of home or jobs due to natural disasters; crops failing due to heat waves and drought or accelerated sea level rises; and serious health problems.

The stress due to experiencing both catastrophic events and personal difficulties during the first quarter of this century is partly responsible for discontent and lack of trust in the nation.

Today, there exists a movement to abandon democratic government and return to an authoritarian system, abandoning the promise of equality, government of the people, by the people and for the people.

The Declaration of Independence
Revisiting the Rationale

Let's take a look back at what motivated the colonists, Did Independence resolve the colonists' problems? What does it mean to us in our present situation?

For 150 years the Colonists and English government got along very well! It wasn't until King George came into power that selfishness came fully into control and things began to change.

The colonists presented 27 complaints as reasons for why they felt they had to become independent from Britain.

The main complaints were: violation of their individual rights, lack of representation, the revenue from the colonist's taxation going to England rather than to the colonies; Britain's cutting off the colonists' trade with other nations; British soldiers quartered in the colonies without the colonist's permission, and who went unpunished when harming the colonists.

Becoming an independent country took care of most of the problems of 1776. Today our tax revenue benefits the United States, and not Britain. We have complete freedom to trade with other nations. The British soldiers left long ago and are now close allies.

As to individual rights, the most serious problem is lack of representation. While representation of voters has improved since 1775, the structure of the senate (two senators by state without regard to population) according to repeated polling does not reflect the will of the people.

Citizens who live in heavily populated states have the same representation as states with very low populations (two senators). In the past, this helped create a sense of one nation by equal representation from every state, but it has become problematic. It is not one person, one vote.

Minority rule is overprotected and we have a very divided country.

The Colonists directly blamed King George for the authoritarian rule that infringed on the colonist's rights. The colonists realized they would never be granted the full rights of Englishmen. There would be no negotiation on the part of Britain to meet the colonists' demands to be treated equally.

The Declaration of Independence was a declaration of freedom from tyranny, freedom from King George and the legislative body controlled by King George. Democracy was born in 1776 in order to give people back their inalienable rights. They wanted equality, freedom, and fairness.

Giving the country back to King George is not an option nor a goal. King George was an authoritarian king, but we could be headed for someone and something much worse. The promise is still Democracy! We may need to make some adjustments to preserve it. However, we do not want to throw the baby out with the bathwater!

We must not and will not give up our request for equality. That was what the colonists wanted more than anything, and that is what the people of the United States want now more than ever! Equality, freedom and fairness!

The colonists, we the people (us), and many in other lands want our inalienable rights!

While the meanings of the Declaration of Independence words: life, liberty and pursuit of happiness have been weakened and challenged, they are still excellent goals! We don't need to change the wording. We just need to remind ourselves what the words really mean!

Life means living fully. Liberty means living freely.

Freedom is not freedom if it negates another person's freedom. Pursuit of Happiness means doing what's necessary to fulfill one's dreams and desires, meet one's obligations and express one's talents and abilities.

Let's not go back to King George!

Justice, Freedom and Truth Redefined

Given the stress we have handled during the early years of this century and the polarity that is affecting our country there are three other teachings of Grundtvig that would be very helpful in meeting the challenges we are facing.

In addition to the four principals, let us further explore what Grundtvig had to say about Justice, Freedom and Truth. What is Justice? What is Freedom? What is Truth?

Justice?
What is Justice?

Ove Korsgaard cites a quote from Grundtvig about justice: "Freedom for Loki as well as for Thor...On this canonical work rests the People's High School movement."[6]

Loki was a Norse god, an unethical trickster, who could change form or even change gender. Loki is known as the god of lies and deceit, a god who causes great mischief.

Thor is the major Viking god of thunder and the sky; Thor wields a hammer and is the god of Truth. As a child, I never believed in Santa Claus, but I did believe in Thor. Now as an adult, I also believe in Loki as a force.

Grundtvig's statement about freedom for Loki is a statement

---

[6] *Ove Korsgaard, N.F.S. Grundtvig-- A Political Thinker, translated by Edward Broadbridge (Copenhagen, Diof Publishing, 2014.)*

about justice. The statement insists on equal accountability for those who are cunning and untrustworthy as for those who have powerful, honorable positions. The opposite is also true. We must insist on equal accountability for people no matter their financial or social status. Also, in order for there to be justice there must be the same accountability for people who are of a minority race as for those who are members of the majority race. Otherwise, there is no justice. That is what is meant by "Freedom for Loki as well as for Thor!" or "Accountability for Thor as well as for Loki."

Freedom?
What is Freedom

During the height of the Covid-19 Pandemic there were many issues regarding freedom. Quite frankly, some people were nearly ready to go to war regarding wearing masks, getting the vaccine, or staying home from crowded events. Unfortunately, "The Common Good" too often was not a consideration when it came to wearing masks or staying home; compliance could have saved lives. Even deaths of loved ones who disregarded recommendations did not seem to dissuade firm believers from noncompliance.

N.F.S. Grundtvig was adamant about freedom. In my interview with Esben Lunde Larsen, a member of the Danish parliament at the time of the interview, described Grundtvig's view on freedom as "Only he can be free who allows his neighbor to be equally free."[7] Grundtvig insisted on reciprocal freedom and

---

[7] *This quotation comes directly from Esben Lunde Larsen, a member of the Danish Parliament whom I interviewed on September 11, 2013. Esben did his Master's level thesis on Grundtvig's understanding of freedom. He has a personal interest in*

responsibility of both the individual and the community. We are created by God and we need to offer our neighbors the same existential conditions that we wish for ourselves.

Freedom is not freedom if it negates another person's freedom. We are all interconnected; we are all interdependent.

This concept of freedom must be taken into consideration in regard to gun ownership and in actions affecting climate change. We are interdependent. My actions affect you. Your actions affect me. This applies to climate change more than ever. N.F. S. Grundtvig said, "For freedom is like fire…, and yet when we have too much of it, it causes general destruction!"[8]

Truth
What is Truth?

At the beginning of this book, I mentioned that in our world today, there is a realization that neither communism, nor capitalism, nor socialism nor dictatorships are meeting the needs for humanity. Axel Kildegaard talked about this in a lecture he gave in August 1998. "It is increasingly clear that the blessings of capitalism and the advance of persons and civilization has been accompanied by ruthless exploitation. Although it now appears that Marxism offered some measure of security, a safety net for the workers, and freedom at least for some from economic class oppression, it also resorted to mass deception and exploitation. It is difficult to overstate the abuses that have marked either

---

understanding Grundtvig's legacy and how to prevent it from disappearing in modern times

[8] *The Danish and The French Revolution, The Common Good edited by Edward Broadbridge and Ove Korsgaard, Aarhus University Press, 2019*

camp."[9]

Axel quotes Dean Allchin of Wales, who believes that Grundtvig speaks like no one else to our era and quotes the Bishop of Coventry in England. "Unless we can find a third way, collaborative and interdependent, especially for the weakest and the poorest, we shall never begin to discover a more satisfying way of life."

Grundtvig's principles and concepts are collaborative and interdependent. Grundtvig's full mantra is "Human First, then Christian". It seems fair to add " or other religions" given our modern, muti-religious world.

Truth requires humanity to have linkage to the divine.

---

[9] *"Church and Life" Vol. LVIII, Number 4, April 15, 1999*

Grundtvig's "Matchless Discovery," "The Living Word"

Grundtvig's "matchless discovery" – the "Living Word," refers to the historical and human word as well as communication from God — is older than the Bible.

The relationship between God and humanity, including communication from the "Living Word," came before the Bible. As someone once explained to me, the Bible is on the altar, the altar is not on the Bible.

The "Living Word" is about the very essence of life. It is more than writings found in a book. It has energy and current meaning. It allows us to comprehend our being; it speaks to our longing for meaning within community. It is where we find Truth with a capital "T".

Grundtvig saw such a way of life at its core as a gift from God. The heart of that gift is what makes all of life and a relational community possible. In the "Living Word" humanity has a linkage to the Divine... a creative inner bond which is also the parent of society and culture...": Every human being can be an ethical person and can make contributions to humanity and society. He or she knows and follows "truths." All human beings can make good choices, practice equality, enjoy nature, learn, contribute to society and be happy!

However, to know Truth, a human being must be open to what Grundtvig names the "Living Word." This sometimes occurs in a person's religious life, but is not limited to any one particular religion, and sometimes is experienced in other ways. To fulfill our humanness, is to become attune to Truth, to experience the "Living Word."

I believe these experiences of "Truths" occur often and to many people. The Declaration of Independence of the United States of America was inspired by the "Living Word."

Although we have known difficult times since this new millennium began, we are making progress toward a more humane world, one for which we are grateful and celebrate life! Let us continue to fulfill our purpose, to establish a country of the people by the people for the people!

Let's not give up on equality! We will not give up on humanity! We are interdependent on each other!

Love Life!

Love Nature!

Love People! – all races, ethnicities and creeds! Empower women!!

Love Lifelong Learning!

Together, let's co-create a new world! Embrace freedom, justice and truth. Recognize the divinity in each other! Manifest equality! We're interdependent!

We are all from the same source!

WE ARE ALL ONE!

PART III:

PROSE POEMS

The Declaration of *Inter*dependence

Inspiration

Meditation

Summation

Finale

In knowing, supporting,

honoring and celebrating

equality, we actualize

individuality and

regain our humanity.

Neither economic power

nor military strength,

the undoing of empires,

assures grandeur.

Allegiance to

human equality

produces greatness.

ARE WE REALLY EQUAL?

Black/white
Yellow/red?
Southern/northern?
Eastern/western?
Slaves/owners?
Men/ women?
Natives/refugees?
Poor/rich?
Well/sick?
Politicians/voters?
Clergy/atheists?
Saints/sinners?
Soldiers/terrorists?
Students/professors?
Strong/weak?
Disabled/able?
Celebrities/unknowns?
Buyers/sellers?
Warriors/chiefs?
Beautiful/ugly?
Ignorant/intelligent?
Old/young?

All essentially equal?

Yep!

Common Denominators

Between birth and

death, disparities

distinguish us.

Life presents

self- correcting

curricula for all,

interminable

learning

permits.

Ways to End Things

Trash it

Mash it

Crash it

Flash it

Bash it

Dash it

Slash it

Gash it

Hash it

Latch it

Cash it

Recycle it?

Time

Time is not days,

minutes, months, years,

decades or centuries.

We have only

Now.

Resolutions

Few tasks are accomplished

alone. Major tasks require

community, collective

spiritual power,

understanding hearts,

emotional heads.

Feel with your brain.

Think with your heart.

We Are not Machines

We are human beings,

A divine experiment,

Grand adventure.

We are not machines!

Each Person

A special conglomerate of

physical, mental and spiritual

traits, gifts, purposes:

DNA, AND

a smidgen of

mysterious, matchless,

illusive essences,

undefined particles,

rare, an embodied

flake of divinity.

Community and Individualism

Often repeated, sometimes
well-heeded,
seldom understood--
individualism needs
community.

We develop our
individuality through
interdependence, find
identity in community.

Without community
there is no identity.
Without interdependence
there is no independence.

Value interdependence,
express individuality,
contribute what you
enjoy sharing,
gain from losing.

Tomatoes

Tomatoes do not have
inalienable rights to
life, liberty and the
pursuit of happiness.

Tomatoes have neither
intellectual nor
emotional
comprehension of
shared tomato-ness,
do not understand
community,
oneness—not
as far as we know.

Tomatoes are not like people.

Connections

Common good threatens

status quo opinions,

leads to exchanges

over differences

and indifference.

At subterranean levels,

all people are in a

universal attempt

to realize common

oneness, merge

fragments of divinity.

Oneness, not Universality

Oneness is not sameness.
The whole is made of discreet
parts.

Sameness is loss of
control, abdication of
responsibility.
Mistrust it.

Oneness is community,
each part separate,
but linked.

Individuality is revelation of
responsibility in community.

Community discourages and
encourages
individuality.

Labeling

Demographic data,

    personal profiles are

        labels, not identity.

History in the Making

Each era
evolves, involves
increased freedom.
Every achievement
counters,
encounters,
rises, falls,
one step back,
two steps forward.

Every tribe, group,
community, individual,handles
scandals.
All people are
created equal.
Every great
movement
knows the truth of
equality.

Our Awakening

Everyone!
Wake up!
Water, sun—
Not resources
to use and
abuse, but
sources of life itself.

Mother Earth is not a
sandbox for building
castles and knocking
them down.
The sand belongs to all!
Share shovels and pails.

Our earth mother is not
a cat's box for disposing
excrement. We have only
one magnificent sandbox!
Keep it tidy.

Earth Mom's Response

Some say,

"She is dying."

Some say,

"It's irreversible."

Some say,

"Every planet

goes sometime."

What does

Earth Mom say?

"Not yet."

Mixed Up

Once we used
things and
loved
people.
Now we
love things
and use
people.
Don't get them
mixed up.

No Accounting

When did office
furniture
become
assets and
employees
become
expenditures?

Resources

OIL and GAS—

Power,

War,

Control,

Separation.

Sources

SUN,

WIND—

Not for sale.

No owners.

Truth

Where there is love there is truth.

Where there is no truth there is no accountability.

Where there is no accountability there is no justice.

Where there is no justice, there is no forgiveness.

Where there is no forgiveness, there is no love.

Where there is truth there is accountability

Where there is accountability there is justice.

Where there is justice, there is forgiveness.

Where there is forgiveness there is love.

Where there is love there is truth.

Redemption

Love the Lord

with all your

heart and all your

mind and all your

soul; love your

neighbor as

yourself.

If you don't

love your

neighbor, and

you don't

love yourself,

you don't

love God.

Remains

Not what you

accomplished;

not what you

 did or didn't;

not money

or possessions.

Legacy equals

how much

love you left,

in your wake.

Actions

A small

action may have

great significance.

A major triumph

may lack value.

Lessons from Grundtvig

Life is not about

competition,

winning,

achieving,

acquiring, or

any particular outcome.

Life is about

being who you are.

Life is about

being thankful and

having loving

relationships.

Life is about

doing what

you are called

to do.

Wealth

Extremely rich,

Extremely poor.

Not much in between.

The middle class is

disappearing, leaving three classes:

poor; sort of poor; very, very rich

with more money than poor and

sort of poor combined.

Successful Countries

A country is more

than its GNP!

People in a truly

wealthy country

are safe,

healthy,

happy,

well- educated,

cared for —and

have a good GNP.

It's Not a Right!

It is not a right
for an 18-year-
old to own an
AR-15 and murder
19 fourth graders
who had the
Right to Life!

It is not a right to
murder 2
dedicated teachers
in their classrooms,
ending their
Right to Pursue
Happiness.

It is not a right
to cause the
deaths of 7
people including
Capital policemen
who had the Right to
Protect Liberty!

THE DECLARATION OF *INTER*DEPENDENCE

Surely even
fourth graders
know such deeds
are not rights! A
right is a wrong
when it takes away
the rights of others.

These are not rights.
No! No! No! No!
Horrendous, tragic
WRONGS!!

(In memory of 21 loved ones who died
at Robb Elementary School, May 24, 2022)

Racial Just Us

We are different flavors:
Awesome! Fabulous!
Equally delicious! Like
slow churned ice cream with
inalienable rights toppings.

You are toasted almond.
He is sea salted caramel.
She is lemon custard.
I am royal dark chocolate.

You are peanut butter crunch.
He is cherry cheesecake.
She is jalapeno vanilla.
I am crunchy coconut.

You are rainbow sherbert.

He is cinnamon papaya.

She is pineapple surprise.

I am chocolate chip cookie dough.

We are different flavors of

human beings with

inalienable rights and

nourishing souls!

Turnings

Around the globe--

Turnings:
east to West
west to East
lies to Truths,
hate to Love
death to Life
dark to Light
blind to Sight
rejection to Acceptance
age to Youth
closed to Open
despair to Joy
owning to Having
alone to With
mine to Ours
scarcity to Abundance
slave to Mastery
I to We
you to Us.

Appendix

N.F.S Grundtvig Biography

Bibliography

Acknowledgements

About the Author

N.F.S. Grundtvig Biography

NF.S. Grundtvig A Short Biography and Statement about
"Grundtvig in America "
by Joy Ibsen

At the Danish American Heritage Society Conference on Danish-American fusion in October, 2017 Joy Ibsen presented on N.F.S. Grundtvig along with Edward and Hanna Broadbridge from Denmark. Hanna began the presentation with comments on Grundtvig's early and foundational influence in Denmark; Edward followed with a discussion of Grundtvig's influence on the fusion of the sacred and secular in Denmark and its past, present, and future relevance. Joy concentrated on Grundtvig's influence in America. This biographical statement on Grundtvig comes from Joy Ibsen's portion of the presentation.

Who was Nicolaj Frederik Severin Grundtvig (1783-1872)? How can we describe this very complex person—as an educator, poet, politician, bishop, theologian, philosopher, hymn writer, or rebel? We can acknowledge the interesting facts beginning with the alignment of the dates of his life with those of the Age of the Enlightenment which might explain why he eventually came to deeply distrust rationalism as the definition of truth. He is known as the father of folk school and even the father of public education in Denmark. Extremely prolific, he wrote or adapted 1500 hymns. His multiplicity and depth as a theologian, philosopher, preacher, philosopher, hymn writer, poet and politician, along with his range of action in personal, political and community life is truly amazing! He was married three times and very involved in the lives of his six children. These are interesting facts, but what was the true significance to Danish Americans? What has been his effect on Danish American Culture?

Ever since 1992 when I heard Walter Capps, an ethics

professor from the University of California Santa Barbara, speak on the "Future of Grundtvigianism," I have seen Grundtvig as a path to a better future more than as a beloved figure of the past. Very briefly, Capps described the unique contributions of Grundtvig to be four intertwined principles which can be followed by almost every human being regardless of religion, race or background:

1. Affirmation of life—Life is good!
2. Stay as close to nature as possible; we are part of nature
3. Ordinary people are good and beautiful (egalitarianism)
4. Lifelong learning and education.

What is now obvious to me is that the holistic combination and intertwining of all four of these principles is what makes Grundtvig unique. Other world leaders have lifted up one or more of the principles—but to honor each and all of these principles in our individual and community lives is what makes the difference. All four principles are accessible to everyone regardless of religion.

We can learn much about Grundtvig from his relationship to his three wives. His first wife, Elisabeth Christina Margrethe Blicher (1787-1851), known as Lissa, supported him through the toughest years of his life, giving him four children and forty years of loyalty. It seemed scandalous to many of his followers when Grundtvig married his second wife, Marie Toft (1813 - 1854), a wealthy widow thirty years younger than he, within a year of Lissa's death, but his relationship with Marie was one of spiritual and intellectual equality. He wrote beautiful poetry to Marie, but their marriage lasted only three years. Marie died shortly after giving birth to their son, Frederik Lange Grundtvig (1864-1903), who grew up to be very important to the Grundtvigian heritage in the United States. After Marie's death, Grundtvig married Asta Tugendreich Adelheid Reedtz (1826-91), a baroness forty years his junior who considered Grundtvig one of Denmark's greatest assets. At age seventy-six Grundtvig fathered his sixth child and named her Asta Marie Elizabeth after all three of his wives.

Other facts about Grundtvig' life:

Grundtvig wrote the first modern translation of Beowulf.

In 1825 N.F.S. Grundtvig called H.N. Clausen, a Theology Professor, a heretic, who in turn successfully sued him for libel. Grundtvig was fined and placed under censorship (1825-1837).

Grundtvig helped write the 1849 Danish Constitution which protects freedom of religion speech, and the press as well as personal freedom.

He was a member of the Lower House of Parliament for 10 years and became a member of the Upper House at age 82.

He chose not to be a member of any political party. Grundtvig became an honorary bishop (without a diocese) of Denmark.

Grundtvig suffered from serious bouts of depression on several occasions but always recovered.

Grundtvig and Marie's son, Frederik, an ornithologist as well as a clergyman, served as a pastor in Clinton, Iowa for 19 years (1881-1900). His most important contribution was a songbook for the Danish people in America of which there are seven editions. Frederik became very involved in the church controversy which split the Danish Lutheran Church in America in 1893 into two factions, the "happy' and the "holy" Danes, over the interpretation of scripture and the possibility of conversion after death. There is no such division in Denmark. Also, the American Grundtvig-oriented Danish Young People's Society sparked deep controversy over the relationship of fellowship to faith. After being separated for more than 100 years, the churches once divided between "Holy" or "Happy" are both part of the ELCA— the Evangelical Lutheran Church of America.

Grundtvigian folk schools came to the United States between 1870 and 1900 when 120,000 Danes came to the United States. Several folk schools were established, including the well-known schools in Solvang, California; Nysted, Nebraska; Ashland, Michigan; Elk Horn, Iowa and Tyler, Minnesota where Danebod Folk School was established in 1888. The present building was built in 1917 after the first one burned. It is the only original residential folk school building remaining in the United State and today the site of an annual folk meeting and three intergenerational camps built on folk school teaching. Folk Schools is about learning to live, realizing what life is about and finding joy in life and happiness through dancing, singing, and gymnastics, reading, listening and discussing history, literature, mythology as well as current issues. Folk schools recognize that every person has value and help each person realize his or her individual gifts. It is about being part of a community, taking part in democracy and society with a firm belief in the ordinary person and lifelong learning.

Today, in the twenty-first century, the Grundtvigian spirit of the folk schools thrives in family camps at Yorba Linda, California; at West Denmark, Wisconsin; and Danebod Folk School in Tyler, Minnesota, which has three family camps as well as a folk meeting for older adults.

One more aspect of Grundtvig's influence, with worldwide significance, can be referred to as "Grundtvig at Harvard." In 2012 I attended a conference on "Grundtvig and Nation Building" which was held at the Harvard Center for European Studies. Scholars have studied failed nations, and now they are looking at what is needed to build successful nations. Frances Fukuyama gave the keynote address on Grundtvig's contributions. While economy and security are high on the list, a successful nation must have much of what Denmark has built as a country, primarily because of Grundvigian priorities—the health and happiness of an educated and civically egalitarian, involved public. While the name of N.F.S. Grundtvig is not well-known in the United States, the influence of Grundtvig in America should not be underestimated.

The Bridge: 41-2 (Fall 2018)

Bibliography

Series: N.F. Grundtvig Works in English
Aarhus University Press, Denmark

Vol 1: The School for Life, N.F.S. Grundtvig on Education for the People (2011)

Vol 2: Living Wellspring, The Hymns, Songs and Poems of N.F.S Grundtvig (2015)
Edward Broadbridge, Translator and Editor; Clay Warren, Editor; Uffe Jonas, Editor

Vol 3: Human Comes First, The Christian Theology of NF.S. Grundtvig (2018)
Edward Broadbridge, Translator and Editor

Vol 4: The Common Good. N.F.S. Grundtvig as Political and Contemporary Historian (2019)
Edward Broadbridge, Translator and Editor, Ove Korsgaard, Editor

Vol 5: The Core of Learning. The Philosophical Writings of N.F.S. Grundtvig (2022)
Edward Broadbridge, Translator and Editor

The Essential N.F.S. Grundtvig (2019),
Anders Holm, Translated by Edward Broadbridge, filo. Dk,

N.F.S. Grundtvig—as a Political Thinker (2014)
Ove Korsgaard, Translated by Edward Broadbridge, DJOF Publishing, Copenhagen.

Acknowledgements

My special thanks to Walter Capps for identifying four Grundtvigian principles which everyone, regardless of religious beliefs or affiliation, can practice, enjoy and celebrate. What a wonderful world it is —and will always be—when we love life, nature, ordinary people and engage in lifelong learning! I wish Walter was still here to help us value each other, and to cheer on our interdependence!

My grateful thanks to Michael Schelde, Hanna and Edward Broadbridge, other helpers, and the 32 persons I interviewed about Grundtvig's relevance in Denmark and modern culture.

My deep appreciation to Brad Busbee and Anders Holm for directing the 2018 Symposium in London about Grundtvig's international influence, and all who supported and participated in "Lands of the Living."

To Danebod Folk School and all who for 75 plus years came to support and enjoy folk school benefits. My deep gratitude to all venues where the development of this powerful "folk school" energy continues to nourish souls, hearts and bodies. Thank you, Dick Juhl, a columnist for Church and Life, who named his column " In the Rear View Mirror." I have drawn from the title as a way of "looking back" in this book.

Thanks to my wise parents, excellent teachers and faculty, and to ethical writers and truthful politicians who taught me the value of democracy. Extreme gratitude to my children Thea, Mitch and Noah for their valuable input and technical support.

A special thanks to the fellow Vineyard writers' group (Delora and Bob Saviteer, Margaret Tessler, Bill Cissna, Jannie De Angelis, and my husband, Don Lenef) for their ideas, feedback, and encouragement as I shared my journey in writing this book.

Thanks to all who keep our democracy going!

THE DECLARATION OF *INTER*DEPENDENCE

I am thankful to live in the Vineyard, a community where we say the "Pledge of Allegiance" at our monthly business meetings. "One nation, indivisible, with freedom and justice for all."

Joy Marie Ibsen—

October, 2022

About the Author

Joy Ibsen lives in sunny, urban Albuquerque, New Mexico, having moved in 2018 from Michigan' Upper Peninsula where she and her husband, Don Lenef, lived on the shores of Lake Superior next to Porcupine Mountains Wilderness State Park. They previously resided in Trout Creek, Michigan, and Oak Park and Evanston, Illinois.

Ibsen has published several other books: *Unafraid*, the second edition, was published in the summer of 2022 with 12 new chapters which take place during the pandemic in 2020-2021. Her other books are: *Here and Hereafter, the Eternity Connection, Songs of Denmark, Songs to Live By; and Poetry in the Porcupines*.

Joy's work is infused with Danish-American culture, values and spirit—particularly the work of N.F.S. Grundtvig the Danish theologian, educator, politician, hymn writer, poet and politician. For 14 years she edited the periodical *Church and Life,* which features Grundtvigian perspectives of life and religion. In 2013 Joy spent two months in Denmark, studying Grundtvig's relevance to modern culture.

Her varied career includes: caseworker in Chicago's Wood Lawn ghetto; teacher of GED to Vietnam bound soldiers at Fifth Army Headquarters, Chicago: English and literature teacher at St. Katherine's /St Mark's preparatory School in Davenport, IA; chief planner for the Model Cities program in Rock Island, IL; director of government relations for Illowa United Way; grant writer/fundraiser for the Greater Milwaukee United Way; fundraising and management consultant to not-for-profit organizations. She served as Development director or Vice President of Development at three Chicago hospitals: Mount Sinai, Bethany Methodist and Swedish Covenant Hospitals. She has a lifelong interest in music; she gave piano lessons and was a church organist in Michigan's UP.

Joy grew up in Danish American Communities in Minnesota, Iowa and South Dakota. She graduated from high school in Viborg, South Dakota, attended Grand View University in Des Moines, Iowa, and graduated from Shimer College (now part of North Central College in Naperville, IL). She pursued graduate studies in Religion and Literature at the University of Chicago Divinity school where she had two classes with the famous theologian, Paul Tillich. Joy has a certificate in Lay Ministry from the School of Theology, University of the South.

For more than 40 years, Joy has devoted time to personal development and spirituality with private teachers including Nancy French, Gwen Osborn, Megan McGeowin and Sai Maa. In December 2022 she was initiated as a Mary Magdalena practitioner.

Joy and her husband have five grown children and five grandchildren.

See website: joyibsen.com